W9-ARV-572

What You Need to Know
About the Economics
of Growing Old*

(*BUT WERE AFRAID TO ASK)

What You Need to Know About the Economics of Growing Old*

(*BUT WERE AFRAID TO ASK)

A Provocative Reference
Guide to the Economics of Aging

Edited by

TERESA GHILARDUCCI

University of Notre Dame Press

Notre Dame, Indiana

Library of Congress Cataloging-in-Publication Data
What you need to know about the economics of growing old (but were afraid
to ask): a provocative reference guide to the economics of aging/edited by
Teresa Ghilarducci.
    p. cm.
  Includes bibliographical references.
  ISBN 0-268-02963-6 (pbk. : alk. paper)
  1. Aging—Economic aspects—United States. 2. Old age—Economic
aspects—United States. 3. Older people—United States—Economic
conditions. I. Ghilarducci, Teresa. II. Title.
  HQ1064.U5W483 2004
  305.26—dc22

2004016404

Contents

Part II   The Social Security System

Part IV   Changing Social Norms

Part V   When the Elderly Work for Pay

List of Figures

Introduction

Will you still need me, will you still feed me,
When I'm sixty-four?
—The Beatles, *"When I'm Sixty-Four"*

I am a baby boomer teaching students so young that their generation has not been named by the marketing profession yet. My first-year students at the University of Notre Dame did not know the 1960s song "When I'm Sixty-Four" (in my opinion, one of the Beatles's best songs, although "Eleanor Rigby" is my favorite). These students were born in 1983 and 1984. Instead of teaching them the song, I assigned reports on social security's financial future and other aspects of the economic business of aging.

They were fascinated by social security, this wide-sweeping program that affected all American lives, and they were fascinated that they did not know about it. It was like finding out about photosynthesis or that the earth circles the sun—vital to understanding the quality of life but so ever-present that social security's magnetic influences were invisible. The students knew more about "welfare," which affects only a fraction of Americans. When they found out about social security's rules, they knew this program was not welfare. They wanted to know the details of this program, how the elderly were doing, and what they could expect; and they were worried about children. In fact, by the third week of the semester, we had collected forty-three questions to which they wanted answers. So this group of twelve first-year students in a Social Science Writing Intensive Seminar, 18 and 19 year olds, decided to find the answers. Their work is in this volume, which Eileen Kolman, dean of the First Year of Studies, took the plunge, without hesitation, to support. This research is the first funded by the First Year of Studies. We are deeply grateful to Dean Kolman and hope it lives up to her expectations. My work in the field of aging over the last six years has been made possible by the Retirement Research Foundation of Chicago, Illinois; the Undergraduate Research Opportunity Program of the Institute for Scholarship in the Liberal Arts and the Undergraduate Intellectual Initiative of the College of Arts and Letters at the University of Notre Dame also helped make the publication of this volume possible.

As baby boomers leave the workforce, the additional stress on the nation's old-age support programs may require some adjustment of their costs and benefits. Or, perhaps, baby boomers will not leave the labor market. Benefit reductions might involve increasing the retirement age, reducing cash benefits, and increasing Medicare cost sharing. Benefit reductions also mean that improving the system to solve old-age poverty is politically difficult. Tax increases could mean expanding the earnings base or increasing the tax rates. Baby boomers may affect job prospects for younger workers. All in all, what is done will affect young people, and what to do fundamentally depends on what the retirement system does for all individuals of all ages and income groups. My students got this.

Notre Dame students have two salient characteristics: they are well-prepared for analytical work, and they aim to be responsible human beings. It turns out marshalling their interests and skills, my goal to introduce new students to economics and to help them learn how to write, edit, and work in a team, and the pertinent questions about the economics of aging created a valuable reference guide for the aging debate.

I was invigorated by my students' wisdom and clarity. I learned more than I thought I ever could. I learned that young women and men fully expect women to have equal opportunities and are sensitive to the needs of children. Many are close to at least one grandparent and are keenly aware of the intergenerational transfers of time, money, and worry that continually occur between adult children and parents. One young woman said repeatedly, "I know what my mother goes through taking care of her mother." Another said, "I didn't have positive feelings about social security until I found out how many people it helps." Another noted that if the elderly have to keep working, there may not be enough quality jobs for younger people and a lot of volunteer time would be lost. Another became keenly aware of how much lower the life expectancy is for lower-income people and African Americans. Another student wondered if we were living longer and better or just hanging on because of abnormal advances in medical care. We figured that other people had these questions, too, so we made this volume. I also found out the answer to my question: "Will you still feed me, when I'm sixty-four?" That answer is here as well.

Teresa Ghilarducci
South Bend, Indiana
July 2, 2003

Part I

The Status of the Elderly

No Exit

*What does it really mean to be elderly and poor;
how does the economic situation of the elderly differ
from the rest of the population?*

The economic situation of the elderly differs from the rest of the population in one simple yet often overlooked way. The retired population lacks opportunity to change their finances. When a person reaches retirement his or her income stabilizes. The social security check always comes once a month, always for the same amount (adjusted for the cost of living only), and it may or may not be supplemented by other outside earnings. You are not likely to hear of seasonal bonuses, raises, promotions, or job offers in the "65 and Older Club." This is because many elderly are either unable or unwilling to work; or, if they do work, it is in part-time positions that do not offer many perks or paths to advancement. Unfortunately, it is usually negative events that interrupt this financial monotony; for example, new medication prescriptions, hospital bills, possibly a death. The relative stability of the elderly's income is noteworthy because although some of the elderly are just as well-off or better-off than the average citizen, those who do run into difficulty or fall into poverty tend to fall harder and stay down longer. In 1993–94 a study specifically directed toward examining entry into and exit from poverty revealed that while the elderly were less likely to become poor, their exit rate was only half that of other adults (14.9% compared to 28.8%). They also had a higher chronic or long-term poverty rate, meaning they were poor for at least twenty-four consecutive months (Naifeh 1998). I attribute these statistics to the aforementioned stability of the elderly's income. They lack the opportunity that comes with being a part of the workforce to increase their wages and pull themselves out of a downward economic spiral.

Single women are a particularly vulnerable subset of the elderly. As of 2001, 21.2% of single elderly women were living below the poverty line, as compared to 15.8% of single elderly men (see figure 1.1). Additionally, one-third of single elderly women are within 125% of the poverty rate. Married couples over the age of 65, on the other hand, had a poverty rate of 4.3%. It pays to be married in retirement. The disproportionate poverty rate of single elderly women is an indicator of who is most susceptible to changes in the social security system. Single

Fig. 1.1 Elderly Living Below the Poverty Level

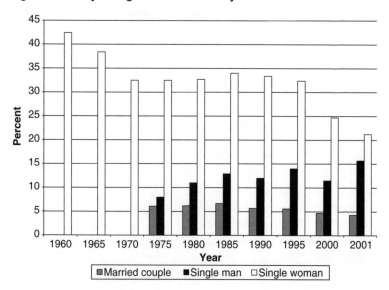

Fig. 1.2   Distribution of Elderly Income by Quintile

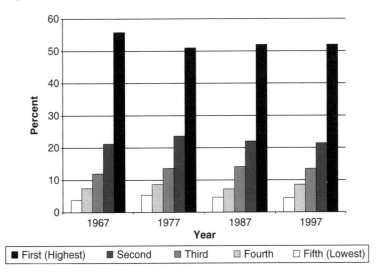

women over 65 rely heavily on social security; for a quarter of these women, social security is their sole source of income (Social Security Administration [SSA] 2002f). Changes in the system involving reduction of benefits would send these women plummeting into poverty with very little chance of escape.

The story of the elderly's income is definitely one book that must not be judged by its cover. The median income for elderly males of all races has nearly tripled since 1950. This is the largest growth rate of all age groups over the course of the last fifty years. Income distribution, however, tells a different tale. The distribution of the elderly's income by quintile has not changed significantly over the last several decades. The top quintile continues to hold about 50% of the income, whereas the lowest fifth of people have less than 5% of the income distribution (see figure 1.2). In 1997 nearly three-fourths of the elderly population had an annual income of less than $35,000, and almost 30% had incomes between $10,000 and $20,000. In sharp contrast, about 60% (the middle three quartiles) of nonelderly households had incomes between $20,000 and $75,000. Basically, the income distribution of the elderly is skewed farther toward the lower-income ranges than that of the nonelderly.

The poverty incidence is particularly unfortunate because, as mentioned above, the elderly are less likely to be able to change their low-income status. Once they are in poverty, they generally have no means of changing their income in order to move out of poverty. As the elderly grow older and begin to require more specialized attention, they are unable to afford the care they need. So while those in the highest income quintile are living comfortably, the majority of the elderly population is battling day by day to make ends meet. (Much of the material in this chapter came from the Century Foundation, Social Security Issue Briefs, available online at http://www.socsec.org, and from the SSA 2002f.)

Quality over Quantity

Will future elderly live more mobile and independent lives as they age, or will they become more and more laden with health problems?

It is a known fact that life expectancies are increasing and our elderly are living longer; however, there is still debate about the condition of the elderly's lives. Are we living longer because we are healthier, or are we just prolonging death by lingering in a poor state of health? This will be crucial to the future of the social security system as well as the labor market as the percent of the population that is 65 and above increases. Will the elderly be able to lead active and independent lives? The best way to examine the health and mobility of the elderly is to look at *functional limitations*. Difficulty in performing personal care tasks and simple home management tasks are referred to as functional limitations. Functional limitations measure one's ability to live independently and serve as indicators for health care services (McNeil 2001). The scale used is called the "Activities of Daily Living" (ADL) and usually includes such tasks as eating, dressing, toileting, and getting out of a bed or chair. Functional limitations increase with age. It would make sense that it is the oldest of the old who have the most difficulty with their daily tasks and functioning. In addition, it is generally women who have a higher percentage of functional limitations in almost every age group. By the time women reach the age of 80, almost 40% require some form of daily assistance, whereas for men of the same age it is only 28% (see figure 2.1). This is compared to about 2% of people aged 15–64. Also, it is interesting to note that these percentages refer to the civilian noninstitutionalized population, meaning that people in nursing homes or other care facilities are not included in the figures.

Debate about the accuracy and relevancy of some of these measurements is fierce. The Instrumental Activities of Daily Living (IADL) index, for example, was developed to assess the ability of people to take part in the more complex tasks of a daily routine. These include shopping, handling personal finances, preparing meals, doing housework, traveling, using the telephone, and taking medication. If these things were included in the ADL, the incidence of elderly requiring assistance would surely be higher. Even so, the data are ambiguous, and different studies often have different results depending on the methods

Fig. 2.1   Elderly Requiring Daily Assistance in 1997

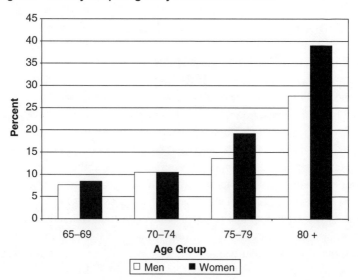

of examination. The overall trend, however, appears to be that functional limitations have been decreasing over the last several decades, and America could, in fact, be on its way to becoming a nation with healthier people. Finally, Americans are realizing the importance of proper nutrition, exercise, the cessation of smoking, and all the other things that make us healthier, especially as we age. Unfortunately, the obesity epidemic may cause an explosion of costs for Medicare because it causes chronic and highly expensive conditions such as diabetes and heart disease. It is essential to form good habits now that we will carry with us throughout life and that eventually will add to a comfortable, healthy retirement.

The Life Expectancy
of the Elderly

What is the average projected life expectancy of the elderly?

Social security is a social insurance system that, among other things, insures against a person outliving his or her savings. Increasing life expectancy, then, would mean that people have more years in which to outlive their savings. This creates a problem in that more people will become more dependent on the insurance offered by social security. Since the beginning of the twentieth century, the average life expectancy at birth for both men and women has increased by over 25 years, from 49.2 years in 1900 to 76.5 years in 1997. Much of this increase, however, most likely was caused by the decrease in the mortality rates among infants thanks to technological advances in medicine and better overall public health. Still, an increase of this magnitude is an appropriate cause for concern when determining the cost of the social security system.

While the data for life expectancy at birth will help to predict future life expectancy, the life expectancy of the elderly once they have reached age 65 is more relevant to the social security issue. The average life expectancies for people at ages 65 and 85, respectively, have also increased alongside the average life expectancy at birth. In 1900 a person who lived to age 65 could expect to live another 11.9 years.

Someone who lived to age 85 could expect another 4 years of life. In 1997 the average 65 year old could expect to enjoy another 17.7 years of life, roughly 6 more years than a 65 year old in 1900. An 85 year old, likewise, had 6.3 years in average life expectancy, 2.3 more than in 1900 (see figure 3.1). When multiplied by the average benefit amount paid by social security and by the number of retired people in the nation, these additional years of life could provide quite a burden on social security, especially since the normal retirement age remains, for the most part, fixed (SSA 2002b).

Since the beginning of the American social security system in the mid-to-late 1930s, the average life expectancy for a 65-year-old person has risen by about 5.5 years, while the normal retirement age has risen just two years, from age 65 for those born prior to 1937 to age 67 for people born after 1960. The social security system needs to be prepared to handle this burden, or the consequences could be serious.

Fig. 3.1   Average Life Expectancies

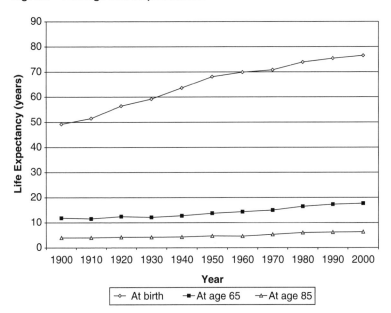

Elderly Poverty: Higher Than You Think

Do the elderly escape poverty? Are poverty measures an accurate assessment of minimum life expenditures?

If somebody's total income is less than the poverty threshold, then one is legally considered poor. But how does one calculate official thresholds? The poverty threshold corresponds to the dollar amount that is deemed adequate to obtain minimum necessary goods and services to sustain life for a short period of time. As far back as Adam Smith's observation in *The Wealth of Nations* (1776), economists have observed that commodities are indispensably necessary for life and those goods that the culture and customs of a country determine to be indecent if one has to do without. Shoes in summer may not strictly be necessary, but they are considered necessities in most industrialized nations.

The official U.S. poverty measure was developed along these lines, although only one "necessity"—a minimum diet—was specified; subsuming other necessary consumption, the smallest amount of money needed is determined as the cost of the minimum diet multiplied by three. In the early 1960s, economist Mollie Orshansky estimated the first poverty thresholds. She knew from the Department of Agriculture's 1955 Household Food Consumption Survey that families of three or more persons spent about one-third of their after-tax income on food in 1955. Accordingly, she calculated poverty thresholds by taking their minimum cost for food and multiplying it by three. She then differentiated her thresholds not only by family size but also by farm/nonfarm status, the sex of the family head, the number of family members who were children, and age status. The result was a detailed matrix of 124 poverty thresholds. Each year the Census Bureau updates the poverty threshold for inflation using the Consumer Price Index (CPI-U).

Poverty guidelines are the other version of the federal poverty measure. They are a simplification of the poverty thresholds and are sometimes loosely referred to as the "federal poverty level" (FPL). They are issued each year in the Federal Register by the Department of Health and Human Services (HHS) and are used for administrative purposes (for instance, determining financial eligibility for certain federal programs) (see U.S. Department of Health and Human Services 2002).

In 2001 the Census Bureau reported that the total population of the elderly was 31,877,000; 10.1% of it (or 3,219,577 people) were living below the official poverty level of $8,494 per year ($708 per month). We must ask, is this a sufficient yearly income? Figure 4.1 shows that alternative measures of poverty yield higher percentages of elderly living in poverty.

Fig. 4.1 Percentage of Elderly Living in Poverty According to Varying Computations

Official poverty level:		10.1		
MSI-NGA :		16.1	MSI-GA :	15.5
MIT-NGA :		13.7	MIT-GA :	12.7
CMB-NGA :		17.1	CMB-GA:	16.2
MSI	=	Medical out-of-pocket expenses (MOOP) subtracted from income		
MIT	=	MOOP included in the thresholds		
CMB	=	Combined methods		
NGA	=	No geographic adjustment for housing costs		
GA	=	Geographic adjustment for housing costs		

Source: U.S. Bureau of the Census 2002.

There seems to be a gap between the legal status of being above the poverty line and financial ease. Therefore, in order to determine if 10.1% describes the well-being of the elderly, one needs to verify if their needs are satisfied by their income and to compare this value (income/expenses) with the thresholds.

Figure 4.2 shows the evolution of the poverty thresholds for people under and over age 65. The latest data available is for 2002; the threshold is $8,628 per year, or $719 per month. We can see that the absolute value of the poverty threshold has grown continuously every year because of inflation, but today's retiree and a retiree whose minimum need per year was $5,156 ($430 per month) in 1985 have the same purchasing power (they are equally poor). In 2001 the poverty threshold indicates that an income of $8,494 would be sufficient, but the average American over 65 spent $27,714 (or $2,310 per month) (see figure 4.3). Consequently, we need to rethink whether being out of poverty stands for having the least amount of money to survive, or if poverty might be the failure to reach the average standard of living.

Figure 4.3 shows that the key expenses of the elderly are housing (33.75%), transportation (25%), health care (13.5%), and food (12.6%). According to this data, average expenditures per year equal 7.5 times the cost of food (total cost / food cost = 27,714 / 3,740 or [in %] 100 / 12.6 = 7.49), not the 3 times the official poverty threshold assumes. The official poverty threshold does not even follow Orshansky's formula. The poverty level for the elderly according to Orshansky's formula would be the food cost ($3,740) multiplied by three, equaling

Fig. 4.2   Poverty Thresholds over Time

		1985	1990	1995	1998	1999	2000	2001	2002
1 person	Under 65	5,593	6,800	7,929	8,480	8,667	8,959	9,214	9,359
	65 AND OVER	5,156	6,268	7,309	7,818	7,990	8,259	8,494	8,628
2 persons	Under 65	7,231	8,794	10,259	10,972	11,214	11,590	11,920	12,047
	65 AND OVER	6,503	7,905	9,219	9,862	10,075	10,419	10,715	10,874

Note: All figures represent people without children.

Fig. 4.3   Average Expenditures of the Elderly in 2001

Type of Expense	65 and over	65–74	75 and over
Housing	9,354	10,629	7,988
Transportation	4,470	5,679	3,177
Food	3,749	4,209	3,255
Health care	3,493	3,583	3,397
Cash production	1,583	1,441	1,734
Personal insurance and pensions	1,157	1,594	690
Entertainment	1,067	1,296	822
Apparel and services	891	1,151	611
Miscellaneous	891	1,189	571
Personal care products and services	396	441	347
Alcoholic beverages	192	233	148
Education	173	201	143
Tobacco products and smoking supplies	154	217	87
Reading	144	159	128
TOTAL per month	2,310	2,669	1,925
TOTAL per year	27,714	32,023	23,099

Note: Amounts are in 2001 dollars.

Fig. 4.4   Ratio of Elderly's Income to the Poverty Level in 2001

Share of the Elderly Population (%)	Elderly Income as a Percentage of the Official Poverty Threshold
2.2	> 50
10.1	100
16.6	125
24.2	150
31.3	175
34.1	180
38.2	200
61.8	<200

Fig. 4.5   Sources of Income for Middle-Income Older Americans

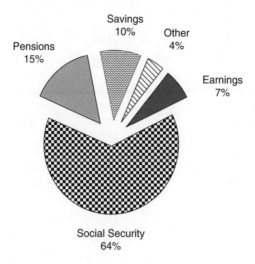

Savings
10%

Other
4%

Pensions
15%

Earnings
7%

Social Security
64%

$11,220; however, the official poverty threshold is only $8,494. It is evident that this threshold is too low. One would need more than twice as much to reach the average consumption. As a result, we might consider as poor not only the elderly who are living below the poverty line but all elderly who are living below 200% of it. Of course, the size of elderly households has to be considered. In addition, if the elderly feed their grandchildren the poverty threshold is severely underestimated (U.S. Department of Labor 2000).

The average income for an elderly person in 2001 was $15,094. Obviously, this is higher than the reference of $8,494 that is supposed to be sufficient. One might even, on a first look, say that on average the elderly are doing quite well because their annual income is 1.8 times higher than the poverty level. But, as we just observed, twice the amount of the threshold is needed for financial ease (to have the same consumer power as the average consumer), so an income of $15,094 is not enough. Figure 4.4 recomputes the depth of poverty (ratio of income to the poverty level). It shows that 38.2% of the elderly are living below the average consumer standard of living (twice the poverty level) in the United States.

There are two alternatives for improving the actual well-being of the elderly: either their expenses should be reduced (for example, through providing more low-income housing), or their incomes should be increased. But what do their sources of income consist of? The sources of income of the elderly, as displayed in figures 4.5 and 4.6, are social security, pensions, asset income, savings, earnings, and public assistance. Figure 4.6 shows that the lowest quintile obtains more than 80% from social security. In other words, apart from social security, the elderly have a sideline income that is not even equal to one-fifth of the amount of money they receive in social security. They are the ones who are "saved" from poverty (SSA 2002f). In fact, without social security, the poverty percentage among the elderly would no longer be 10.1% but nearly 50%!

Fig. 4.6   Sources of Income for Senior Households by Quintiles of Income

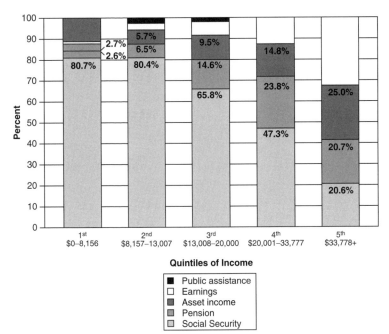

Note: A quintile, statistically speaking, is the portion of a frequency distribution containing one-fifth of the total sample.

Furthermore, as we already saw, the number of elderly living in financial need is larger than the number of people living under the poverty level.

Figure 4.6 also shows that the richest quintile's income consists of only 20% from social security. The term "greedy geezer" was coined about a decade ago to refer to those seniors and retirees who were financially secure but continued to accept social security payments and other entitlements (approximately the top 5% of the elderly). They do not need social security as a sideline income and, furthermore, the dissolution of their benefits would likely profit their younger, disgruntled counterparts. The elderly's representation in Washington, however, protects them from dissolution of their benefits.

Because of this highly "media-tized" image of greedy geezers and because the poverty percentage of the elderly is lower than the rest of the American population, one thinks, at a glance, that the elderly escape poverty. But one has to differentiate between assumptions and facts. Furthermore, one should remember that the given numbers concerning elderly poverty are too low in actuality. The official 10.1% of poor elderly are only those who are on the edge of survival. The poverty thresholds should be reformed to adjust further to the elderly's consumer power.

Still, to answer the question of whether or not the elderly escape poverty, one can say that, on the one hand, the average elderly person does escape poverty as evidenced by an average income of more than twice the threshold, but, on the other hand, more elderly than officially measured are living in financial unease.

Big Spenders and Gamblers: The Elderly in Debt

Are the expenditures of the elderly exceeding their incomes?

Perhaps due to the growing number of baby boomers accustomed to a comfortable lifestyle, American seniors are racking up debt like never before. This debt load could cause the nation to fall into a financial crisis and disrupt other nations' economies. According to the Consumer Bankruptcy Project, in 2000 about 82,000 out of 32.6 million (about 0.25%) Americans age 65 or older filed for bankruptcy with an average of $30,000 in debt loads. Over the last eight years, household debt for those 65 and older has skyrocketed 164%; the level reached $20,302 in 2000 (Consumer Expenditure Survey 2003).

This increasing amount of debt shows that many seniors do not handle and manage their finances optimally. Many of them are not prepared for their retirements. Living just within their income before retirement does not help them save enough money for the future. Even though banks pay interest on their CDs and bank accounts, the rates are not high enough for the elderly to keep up with their expenditures. Expenditures include food, housing, utilities, public services, basic needs, and personal insurance.

Two age groups spend more than their income. The first group is consumers under age 25. As expected, young people spend more than

Fig. 5.1   Annual Income after Taxes vs. Expenditures in 2000

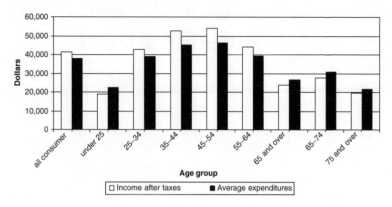

they earn and less than older individuals. (They spend about 40% more than individuals ten to twenty years older.) In fact, every age group but the elderly and the young are savers; that is, they spend less than they earn (net of tax). Spending by people age 65 and over exceeded their incomes by 11% in 2000 (see figure 5.1). For most elders pensions and social security comprise the majority of their incomes after retirement. In 2001 about 44% of retirees claimed that social security was their primary source of income, up from 38% in 2000. Stock investments and bank interest rates have helped them to live on little more than social security. Using their money for medical emergencies, major home repairs, and loans to children and grandchildren, however, could significantly decrease their savings.

Bankruptcy and debt of those 65 and older are caused by various factors. "Trouble keeping up with the bills" is cited in surveys as one of the most common reasons. For example, many medical expenses are being charged to credit cards. According to a report by the Commonwealth Fund, out-of-pocket health care expenses for seniors increased nearly 50% from 1999 to 2001 (Achman and Gold 2002). With a large amount of unexpected medical expenditures and a small amount of benefits from social security, the elderly are not able to make credit card payments. They have to wait until they receive their next social security check, and late fees and penalty interest rates cause their credit card balances to inflate. A study from Harvard University found that nearly half of the elderly who filed for bankruptcy did so because of medical expenses. There are many other minor reasons for the elderly's debt, such as the desire to help family members. Sending money to their children and grandchildren every month increases their overall expenditures. Meanwhile, seniors who cannot handle the increased loneliness and boredom that often accompany old age might seek consolation in gambling. For whatever reason seniors choose to gamble, many have never done so before and are unaware of the problems it can cause. According to the American Psychiatric Association (2003), gambling addiction is defined as an "Impulse Control Disorder"; an estimated 5–7% of the elderly population suffer from this problem. This means that about 1,630,000 elderly people in the United States have gambling problems. About two-thirds (67.8%) of seniors surveyed said they gambled in the past year. Seniors buy lottery tickets, raffle tickets, and scratch and pull tickets. Seniors also play coin slot machines and bingo. Though bingo is the stereotypical activity of the American elderly, only 18% do so, while 77% buy lottery tickets. Seniors typically participate in these activities monthly, and about 40% of seniors who buy lottery tickets and play bingo do so weekly (Hirsh 2000).

Another factor that could cause seniors to have a difficult time managing their expenditures is home equity loans. Due to the rise of home equity loans and second mortgages among elderly Americans, many seniors have financial problems caused by excessive mortgage debt. When elderly Americans take out a high-interest loan that exceeds their income, it becomes a problem. According to Christine Dugas, a writer from *USA Today*, "For many seniors, their only major asset is their home. Although pensions are a protected asset, in most states only a small amount of home equity is protected in bankruptcy. So if the value of the equity exceeds the state exemption, then a person who files for bankruptcy will lose their home" (Dugas 2002).

In order to alleviate bankruptcy and debt problems, many government-supported programs like Medicare and nonprofit credit counseling agencies have been formed. Many older Americans, however, have not sought help from counselors or other programs and have suffered in silence.

Part II

The Social Security System

Old Age and Social Disability Insurance

What percentage of retired beneficiaries receive benefits for their spouses, divorced spouses, and children? What percentage collect Old Age and Social Disability Insurance benefits before retirement? Are there any variations based on race?

Spouses who paid into social security are first and foremost eligible for their own benefits. Those who have not paid into the system may be among the 700,000 people per year who apply for spousal benefits. Under the 2002 spousal benefits policy, a husband or wife who abstains from the workforce to raise a family is entitled to payment equal to half of the working partner's benefit. This benefit comes as a separate check in the noncontributing spouse's name.

Like married spouses, divorced spouses are entitled to their own benefits. If applying for spousal benefits, the divorced spouse is eligible for benefits on the highest earnings record of his/her partner. In order to receive benefits based on the earnings of a divorced spouse, the marriage has to last for a minimum of ten years, and the beneficiary must be at least 62 years old, be unmarried, and not be eligible for an equal or higher benefit on his or her own social security record or on someone else's social security record.

Fig. 6.1 Disability Ratio for Retired Whites

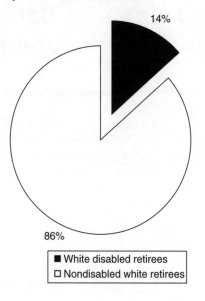

14%

86%

■ White disabled retirees
□ Nondisabled white retirees

Fig. 6.2 Disability Ratio for Retired Blacks

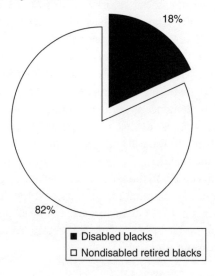

18%

82%

■ Disabled blacks
□ Nondisabled retired blacks

Benefits are available for children of disabled parents. In order for the child to qualify for benefits the parent must qualify for social security disability and the child must either be under the age of 18, be a full-time student under the age of 19 (in grades 1–12), or have a permanent disability that started before the age of 22. Social security represents an important part of income for millions of children. Most of the young families receiving financial assistance from Old Age and Social Disability Insurance (OASDI) are poor or near poor. All told, social security paid over $14 billion dollars to children in 2001. Over five million children under the age of 18 earn part of their family's income through social security payments. This is equal to about 5% of all U.S. children. These numbers are significant because they show the impact that social disability insurance has on young families. It is important to remember that the OASDI provides $250,000 dollars of insurance for a normal working family. The group most likely to collect this insurance is African Americans. Because black males are more likely to become ill or disabled at a younger age, there is a larger representation of their children in the system. African American children represent 15% of the U.S. population under the age of 18, yet they receive 23% of social security's children's payments (SSA 2002f). This figure is proportional to the number of disabled blacks that have exited the workforce due to injury or illness (see figures 6.1 and 6.2).

Paying Your Dues

*How much money does the average retiree contribute
to social security in a lifetime?*

Since payments for social security come from taxes taken directly out
of the paychecks of workers, it makes sense to look at wage rates when
discussing the average contributions of retirees. These contributions
can vary directly with the average wage rates or average annual earnings. If wages are higher in a given year, then social security contributions for that particular year will naturally be higher, unless the government makes changes to Old Age and Social Disability Insurance
(OASDI) tax rates.

The government *has* made changes to the tax rate since 1937, so
these changes must be taken into account by multiplying the wage
rates by the tax rate of a given year to find that year's average social
security contribution (see figures 7.1 and 7.2). After this has been
done, the data can be analyzed. A robust, healthy growth in social
security contributions is desirable. This means that the amount of
money going into the social security system is sufficient to cover the
costs of benefits, which grow as more people retire and live longer.

If, on the other hand, there is little or no growth in the amount of
average social security contributions, then social security is "outgrowing"

Fig. 7.1   Old Age and Social Disability Insurance Tax Rate

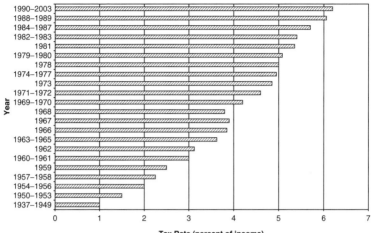

Fig. 7.2   Average Annual Income

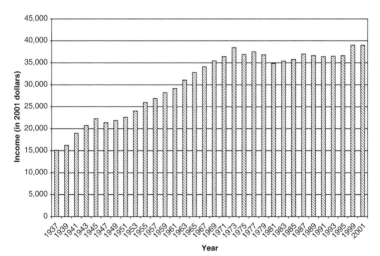

the funding being put into the system, and it will eventually run dry. If the data shows a decline in the average contribution to social security, then it is time to panic, because the gap between social security contributions and benefits is widening by an increasing factor. In these last two scenarios, money would need to come from other sources to cover the deficit in social security. In other words, the money for the retirees' benefits would need to come from workers in the younger generations.

Thankfully, as the data for the United States' social security system indicates the average worker's contribution to social security has been climbing fairly steadily, and sometimes rapidly, since 1937 (see figure 7.3). Both OASDI tax rates and average income have experienced significant growth. OASDI tax rates have increased by 5.2% (from 1% of income in 1937 to 6.2% in 2003). Likewise, average annual salaries have increased from $15,111 in 1937 to $38,982 in 2001, an increase of $23,871 (all figures are in 2001 dollars). When these figures are combined, it yields an increase of $2,265.77 in average social security contributions per worker since 1937. This is good news for the system, because it means that social security contributions are climbing alongside the increasing amount the system will have to pay in benefits.

Fig. 7.3   Putting It Together: Average Worker Contribution to Social Security

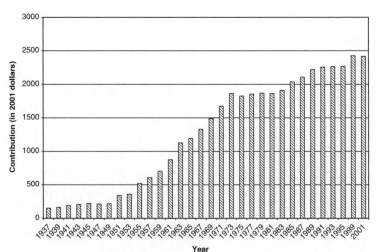

Also, since contributions in the present are so much higher than they were in the past, it means there will be enough money to reimburse current retirees. This data is dependent on employment and productivity, however, since average annual income can only increase if employment is constant. In the early 1980s there was a decrease in salaries. An increase in the OASDI tax in the late 1980s was necessary to correct this problem. This means that a trend of increasing salaries and OASDI taxes cannot in and of themselves ensure a successful future for the social security system (SSA 2002f). Productivity and employment must also be strong to ensure the system's future success. Reform is obviously needed, although this is hardly surprising because the system design depends on continual updates.

Reaping the Benefits

How have social security replacement rates changed over time?

The replacement rate is the percentage of a retiree's pre-retirement income that social security is able to replace. Because the rate varies among people of different income levels, the replacement rate is a good example of the progressive nature of the social security system. For example, in 2000 the low earner received 55.5% of his pre-retirement earnings in the form of social security, the medium earner 41.2%, and the maximum earner 27.3% (see figure 8.1). These rates are projected to decrease across the board by 2030. This is important for those planning to retire within the next thirty years because it appears that the role of social security is declining. People will be forced to turn to other sources of income to make up for what social security cannot provide.

The replacement rates of the past are rather interesting. In the retirement year of 1950 the average replacement rate was 35%, and it hovered right around this level for about twenty years. In 1972 a law was passed to provide automatic cost-of-living adjustments to all social security recipients. The point of these COLAs, as they were called, was to make sure that benefits kept pace with inflation. Unfortunately, there was a flaw in the formula that determined COLAs that actually caused benefits to increase faster than inflation. This had the unintended effect of substantially increasing replacement rates for the next five years until the mistake was corrected in 1977. Consequently, a small cohort of people received quite a windfall; namely, those people born between the years 1910 and 1916 whose benefits were determined according to the flawed formula. In order to ameliorate an abrupt change for those about to retire when correcting this mistake, a special "transition" formula was used to calculate benefits for the next five years. This period saw a pullback in replacement rates of more than 10%, which left many Americans griping about the fairness of the situation. This period was called the "notch" and, in fact, was not intentionally unfair. No one was receiving less than they should have; however, a few lucky elderly were receiving a little extra. After the effects of the botched COLA attempt had been felt and then remedied, the replacement rate settled right around 42%, which is where it is today for the medium earner. (Data in this chapter is from SSA 2002f.)

Fig. 8.1   Social Security Replacement Rates at Age 65

Year	Low Earner	Medium Earner	Maximum Earner
2000	55	41.2	27.3
2030	49.1	36.5	24.0

Note: As percentage of income.

Who Stands to Gain

*What is the expected payout of social security benefits for
women and African Americans? Who lives to
collect these pensions?*

Women are the most numerous beneficiaries within the social security
system, based upon the availability of spousal benefits and the fact that
the average woman lives longer than the average man. A woman who
reaches age 65 in the year 2000 is expected to live 19.2 years beyond
that, which would make the average woman 84.2 years of age at her
death. The average male turning 65 in 2000, however, is expected to
live only another 16.3 years, which would put his death at the age of
81.3 years. This gives the average women 19.2 years to receive full
social security benefits—2.9 more years of benefits than the average
male. As of December 2001, there were 12,676,620 women receiving
social security benefits, so clearly women make up a large portion of
beneficiaries.

With women living longer than men and, therefore, spending more
time within the parameters of social security, women take in a large
share of the benefits paid out within the system. According to the
Social Security Administration, in 2000 the average monthly benefit for
women was $729.60. If this number was the same today, a woman who

lived until the age of 84.2 would receive approximately $167,808.00 during her retirement years (SSA 2002f). This income is spread out over 19.2 years (if the woman begins receiving full benefits at the age of 65) and is a considerable amount of money, especially when you consider that elderly women rely on social security more than any other group. According to the National Center for Policy Research for Women and Families (n.d.), "Women depend more on social security because they are less likely than men to have their own private pensions when they retire."

Life expectancy plays a key part in the social security system because the longer a person lives, the more benefits they receive and, thus, a greater amount of money must be taken from the system. Because white women live 5.2 years longer than white men (see U.S. Bureau of the Census 2002), and the average female lives 5.4 years longer than the average male, females are receiving benefits for a longer period of time than men. Because they are living longer, women are usually on their own during the later stages of their lives. As a lone income recipient, they are exposed to the risk of poverty.

These numbers vary even more for African Americans, particularly African American women. The average African American has a shorter lifespan than his/her white counterpart. According to the U.S. Census Bureau's statistics, the average African American female lives 4.6 years less than the average white female, and the average African American male lives 5.9 years less than the average white male. These disparities are quite large and result in African American workers receiving benefits for fewer years than white workers.

As of December 1998 the average monthly payout for African American men age 65 to 69 was $734.20 a month. For African American women the monthly payout was $584.60, considerably lower than the payouts for women in general. Not only are African American men and women receiving benefits for a shorter period of time, the benefits they do receive are less than their white counterparts.

Redistribution of Wealth

Do lower-income workers receive relatively less from social security?

Lower-income workers naturally receive a lesser amount of social security benefits than workers with higher incomes because they contribute less to the system than workers who earn higher wages during the thirty-five-year earning period. However, lower-income workers receive a higher replacement rate than any other group of workers (see figure 10.1). Despite the high replacement rate for lower-income workers, they are still in a worse position than middle- and high-class workers due to their low earnings throughout their working lives. Social security does not make the poor richer and the rich poor.

A worker in the lowest 20% of household income will get back about twice as much in benefits as he pays in taxes. Because this amount is spread out over the number of years spent in retirement, the benefits low-income workers receive are not sufficient to sustain an adequate standard of living. The poor, particularly the working poor (those who work throughout their lives to contribute to social security but still fall below the poverty line), are extremely vulnerable within the current social security system.

The 2001 replacement rate, according to the Economic Opportunity Institute, is approximately 57% for a low-wage earner (Watkins 2001). Social security benefits for the year equal $7,992, compared to $14,000 in actual earnings. The replacement rates decrease as income increases. For a worker earning the median wage, the replacement rate is 41%, with $13,848 in benefits, compared to $34,000 in actual earnings (see figure 10.1). For a worker earning a high wage, the replacement rate is 23%, with benefits equaling $18,432 compared to $80,400 in actual earnings. As you can see, the rate of replacement decreases as income increases, but the lower the replacement, the higher the yearly social security benefits (see figure 10.2) (SSA 2002f).

Another factor that affects low-income earners is life expectancy and the mortality rate. Low-income earners tend to live shorter lives than higher-income earners, and, therefore, they do not collect benefits for as long as higher-income earners. All of these factors expose lower-income earners to more hardship than any of the other cohort groups that pay into the social security system. While social security benefits are the

Fig. 10.1   Sources of Income for Middle-Income Older Americans

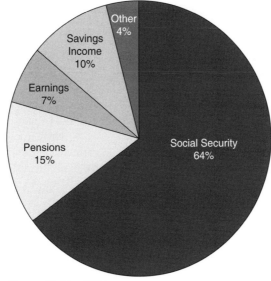

Source: Watkins 2001.

Fig. 10.2   Expected Annual Social Security Benefits for Elderly Retiring at Age 65

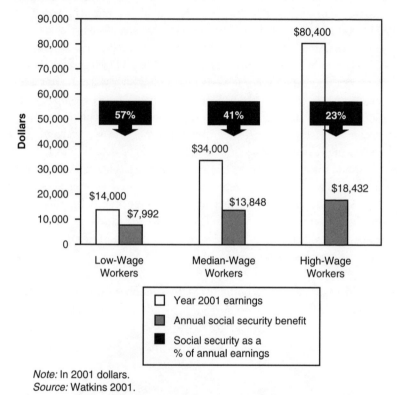

Note: In 2001 dollars.
Source: Watkins 2001.

primary form of retirement income for low-income earners and despite having the highest replacement rate, for a worker who earned minimum wage his or her entire life, this is not a lot of money. The low-income earners are the most vulnerable of any group within the social security system for all of these reasons. But in respect to their earnings prior to retirement, they receive a higher percentage than any other group, showing that social security is, in fact, a progressive system. This percentage reflects their standard of living prior to retirement better than the replacement rates for the other cohort groups. In this respect, then, they do not receive less from social security, although their benefit payments each month are significantly lower than those who earn higher wages due to the amount that they contribute to the system as a whole.

11

The Freedom to Work Act

How has the Freedom to Work Act affected both the age at which the elderly begin collecting benefits as well as their presence in the workforce?

On March 28, 2000, Congress passed the Senior Citizens Freedom to Work Act (FTWA) with a record 419-0 vote. Signed into law (P.L. 106-182) on April 7, 2000, FTWA eliminated the earnings test for retirees who have attained full retirement age (FRA). This is a fairly radical change to the system. The bill provides for the elimination of the social security retirement earnings test in and after the month in which a person attains full retirement age, now age 65, until age 70. A revised earnings limit is applied to all retirees not between the full retirement age and 70. That limit is now $30,000. Benefits are withheld at the rate of $1 for every three dollars of earnings above $30,000. This earnings limit will be adjusted as average wages fluctuate. Also important is the provision for delayed retirement credits (DRCs). First outlined in the 1983 Greenspan review, DRCs provide for the postponement of any month's payment between the attainment of full retirement age and age 70 for which the worker requests that benefits be withheld. Therefore, a retired person between the ages of 65 and 70 may defer monthly payments as they choose. The delayed retirement credit will increase a retiree's monthly payments after age 70 by two-thirds of 1% per month delayed. This deferral of collection will not increase benefits by more than 8% per year. However, the provision that allows retirees to collect benefits and earn up to $30,000 will increase income possibilities for the elderly. Prior to the passage of the Freedom to Work Act, the earnings level hovered around $17,000.

The Freedom to Work Act did not change the annual exempt amount for beneficiaries below the full retirement age. A beneficiary may choose to collect benefits beginning at the age of 62. The amount paid per year is currently $11,280. It remains indexed to average wage. The withholding penalty is also greater if early collection is chosen; the earnings test is $1 for each $2 of earnings over the exempt amount (currently $30,000).

Though unanimously supported in Congress, the Freedom to Work Act did not pass without debate. Proponents of the act argued for its practicality and fairness, stating that it was unfair to penalize the elderly for working by not giving them their full benefits. An earnings penalty on social security benefits has a negative effect on work incentives, and it can hurt elderly individuals who need to work to supplement their social security benefits. Although the benefit withholdings under the retirement earnings test (RET) are partially recovered through increased benefits once a worker reaches age 70, the RET is viewed as a tax on earned benefits. Eradicating the RET has two potential effects: (1) some people may choose to remain in the workforce or to continue to work full-time because they would not face the same reduction in their current social security benefits; and (2) some people may choose to work less, making up for lower earnings with higher current social security benefits. Opponents of the Freedom to Work Act argue that the retirement earnings test is an appropriate measure for the execution of social security. Intended as a social insurance program, social security should only protect workers from the loss of income due to retirement, death, or disability of the wage earner. Eliminating the retirement earnings test might alter the risks that beneficiaries face as they grow older, creating more incentive to retire early and save less. Currently 60% of workers choose to receive benefits at the minimum retirement age of 62. Using this logic, opponents consider it appropriate to withhold benefits from workers whose substantial earnings show they have not in fact retired.

Growth of Beneficiaries vs. Contributors

How is the number of beneficiaries changing over time in comparison to the number of contributors, and what essential effects are these growth rates inflicting on the system?

It is evident that both beneficiaries and contributors are consistently rising in numbers, though not at the same rate. It would seem that beneficiaries growing at a greater rate than contributors would automatically result in the system's financial imbalance. However, it is equally important to examine the wage growth rate because it directly affects the amounts contributed. Wages must grow to support the growing number of beneficiaries. I contend that this is not the case; without an increase in taxes, the system will be in deficit in the future.

Beginning with data from 1950, the growth of contributors to the system has been steadily increasing, as well as the number of beneficiaries (see figure 12.1). When the data are charted, however, it becomes evident that beneficiaries grew at a fast rate while the growth of contributors has been somewhat steadier. Still, the ratio of those age 65 or older (beneficiaries) to those ages 20 to 64 (workers) is currently lower than it was in 1950, and it is forecasted to decrease until 2010. Even when the ratio does rise, as it will due to the baby boomers (reaching a ratio of 0.86 in 2080), it will still be lower than the 0.95 level it was at in 1965 (SSA 2002b, Table V.A.2).

The social security equation can help to explain why the system has projected deficits despite the ratio of beneficiaries to contributors not being extraordinarily high. The equation sets expenditures equal to revenues: (Beneficiaries) (Benefit Amount) + Administrative Costs = (Tax Rate) (Wages × Laborers) + (Interest Rate) (Trust Fund). A huge misconception, strongly fueled by the media's and the public's lack of knowledge of the system, is that if beneficiaries are rising in number while laborers are decreasing, the system will be thrown out of balance and end up in debt. Hence the fear that when the baby boomers retire and cause a huge decrease in contributions and, simultaneously, a huge increase in benefit payments, the system will run out of funds. This is not the case, however.

The social security actuaries foresaw the effect the baby boomers would have on the system. Their presence has been planned for many years. Beneficiaries and wages are on opposite sides of the above equation. Thus, actuaries predicted that as time passes and the number of beneficiaries increases, wages will increase. Essentially, an economy that is growing should be increasing its productivity. When productivity increases, this should be reflected by increasing wages. So when the number of beneficiaries increases, actuaries are banking on higher

Fig. 12.1   Growth Rates of Beneficiaries and Contributors

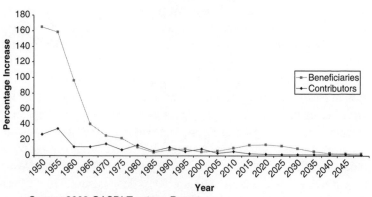

Source: 2003 OASDI Trustees Report.

wages due to economic growth to keep the system in balance. The problem lies in the fact that neither productivity nor wages have increased at the anticipated rate, thus throwing the equation out of balance.

So the question that surfaces next is, Why are productivity and wages not growing? Productivity is defined as the ratio of real gross domestic product (GDP) to hours worked by all workers. Productivity increased greatly in the 1990s with the technology boom, and forecasters readily predicted continued growth at such rates. This did not occur, however, due in part to a slowdown in the computer hardware market (Gist and Verma 2002). In their report for 2003, the Social Security Administration (2002b) predicted rates of productivity growth to be the same as they were in the 2002 report, implying no new expected declines. However, the report predicts a decrease from 3.6 in 2002 to only 1.9 in 2003, followed by a predicted increase to 2.3 in 2004. The report states that these predictions represent the slow growth of the last quarter of 2002 and the forecasted accelerated growth into 2003. After 2003, the report says, the change in productivity will decelerate to the predicted 1.6 in 2011.

Dependents: Mouths to Feed

How many "mouths" do workers today feed? What is the ratio of dependents to workers?

Dependents of a worker can be considered as the number of "mouths" a worker must feed. These dependents can be children who are too young to have a job, elderly who are retired, or other individuals between the ages 20 and 64 who are not employed. A large group of these nonworkers are spouses. All of these dependents rely on the worker as a source of income. These dependents are also covered for insurance purposes by social security. I suggest that the value people place on social security is in direct correlation to the number of dependents workers feed.

Different areas of social security have been important during different eras in its history. Since more and more families have both husband and wife working, the spousal dependency provision is not as important as it was in earlier time periods. In fact, it has been on the decline in recent years because more women are working jobs covered by social security. Spousal dependency is not completely obsolete, however; even with more women working, being dependents of their husbands could earn them more money from social security. Previously, women needed to be dependents of their husbands because their work did not earn them enough money, if any. This can be seen from look-ing at the makeup of unemployed persons between the ages of 20 and 64. In 1950, 87% of the nonworker dependents between the of ages 20 and 64 were women. This number declined as more women entered the workforce over time. In 1980 the percentage decreased to only 53%. Starting around this time, the percentage leveled off and re-mained at about 60% for the rest of the data, projected until 2050 (Reno and Olson 1998, 7). This shows that the influx of women into the workforce has stabilized.

Child dependents are declining, meaning that the average family size has been shrinking (see figure 13.1). Family size when the baby boomers were children was much larger than it is now. This means that

Fig. 13.1   Dependents per Worker

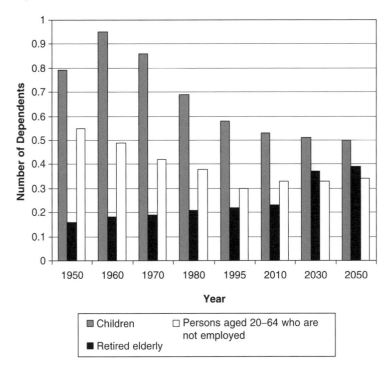

the overwhelming number of retiring baby boomers will not have as drastic an effect as people think. Social security will still function because as more people from the baby-boom era retire, workers will have fewer child dependents. Also, the workforce is not expected to shrink, so the number of workers will remain constant (Reno and Olson 1998, 1). This will affect the baby boomers' retirement. People expect the social security system to be incapable of handling the retirement of the baby boomer generation, but this is not a problem. The ratio of total dependents per worker will continue to decrease slowly over the next seventy-five years and will allow the social security system to survive the baby boomers' retirement (Reno and Olson 1998, 3). The number of retired elderly dependents will increase over time as the baby boomers retire, but the total number of dependents per worker will not change drastically from that of previous times. In 1950 the total number of dependents per worker was 1.48, and in 2050 it is projected to be 1.23. This gradual decline will allow social security to survive the baby boomers' retirement.

These statistics also show that people do not have the same reasons for supporting social security. Social security offers many things in its insurance plan. It provides a floor for retirement income, as well as insuring against a loss of income because of disability. It also protects the dependents of the worker in the case of the breadwinner's death. If a worker has many dependents, then he/she is going to value the insurance that social security offers because he/she could possibly die and leave behind these dependents. If the worker knows that they will receive aid from social security, then it makes sense for him/her to support social security.

Workers who have dependents to take care of are more in need of insurance in the case of their death or disability than those without dependents. Social security, therefore, is more important to workers with many dependents than to workers that live on their own without any dependents. The Social Security Administration's Office of the Actuary states that a policy of $207,000 would be needed to duplicate just the disability coverage that social security offers. Another $307,000 would be needed to equal the protection for survivors (Skidmore 1999, 7). Social security is extremely reasonable compared to these prices—it is only 6.2% of a worker's income. Social security provides workers with an affordable insurance plan, whereas the cost of private insurance for these workers would be much greater (Skidmore 1999, 7). Social security would seem to have the most to offer large families and workers with many dependents. It provides workers with a reliable insurance plan, whether they have a family or not. However, the worker with a large family stands to gain the most from social security in the event of death or disability and would value its reasonability the most. All workers, regardless of the number of dependents, pay the same amount into social security (6.2% of their earnings), but the worker with many dependents has a better chance of either himself or his dependents seeing a larger portion of the money sometime in the future.

Do the Old Eat the Young?

How do the amounts of GDP distributed to the elderly (over 65) and the young (under 18) compare, and what are the repercussions of our spending choices?

It is true that the federal government spends more on the elderly. I postulate that social security, coupled with Medicare, creates expenditures far greater than those of any child care programs. I think the spending choices of the federal government have many societal effects, not just the obvious financial aspects but also in terms of the underlying principles that our society values and accepts as norms. However, federal spending is not the only factor that should be examined when trying to understand the spending patterns with regard to the old and young.

An excellent report by John Gist and Satyendra Verma, "Entitlement Spending and the Economy: Past Trends and Future Projections" (2002), covers many, if not all, of the factors determining who is getting more of the government's money in terms of age. It identifies the difficulty in trying to untangle who is getting what and the necessity for researchers to look at not only the expenditures of the federal government but of state and local governments as well. The paper comes to the conclusion that federal benefits are traditionally given out later in life while state and local benefits are given earlier in life. For example, while the elderly receive social security from the federal government, young people are receiving public education as a benefit from state and local governments. Statistics reveal that state and local governments spend about 30% of their total budget on public education, while the federal government is spending 35% on older persons. Thus, once spending by federal, state, and local governments is combined and compared, spending on the old and young is much closer to being equal (Gist and Verma 2002, 14).

First, let us look at the actual spending. Figure 14.1 shows the ten most expensive entitlement programs. The majority are programs for older persons (social security, Medicare, civilian and military retirement, unemployment, supplemental security income, and veterans benefits), while there are only two programs with "direct" benefits to children (child tax credits and family support). Granted, there are many other entitlement programs that benefit children; they are just not among the ten most expensive.

Fig. 14.1   Government Spending on the Ten Most Expensive Entitlement Programs

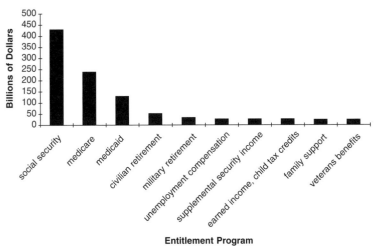

Entitlement Program

Note: In 2001 dollars.
Source: Gist and Verma 2002.

Examining spending at a completely fundamental level reveals that social security and Medicare eat up a relatively large portion of the budget. Thus, in the "Who is the money spent on?" debate, retirees appear to be favored while children are forgotten. The director of the Congressional Budget Office (CBO) testified that 34.8% of the budget is being spent on the over-65 population, while only 8.4% is spent on the under-18 age group. However, these calculations do not illustrate how tax benefits are allocated. Most federal spending benefits are received by the older population, while most federal tax benefits are received by those ages 20 to 64. Finally, the CBO points out the risk of stating that an entitlement benefits one specific age group when ultimately the beneficiaries may be different than they first appear. For example, the social security entitlements given to the elderly may eventually benefit their children because they will not have to spend time and money taking care of their elderly parents (Gist and Verma 2002).

The conclusion, as stated earlier, is that relatively equal amounts of money are spent on the elderly and the young when all levels of government spending are taken into account (granted, slightly more is spent on the elderly). What does this say about our society's values? An obvious answer is that we view youth and old age as equally important. But is this really what we see in society? Does society have more of a problem with putting children in unsafe, unloving daycare situations than it does with putting elderly in unsafe, unhealthy nursing homes? Maybe it would be beneficial to divert some spending from the elderly to the young so that when future generations age, they will not need as much assistance. Judging from personal experience, I have seen my mother spend a lot of time and money taking care of her mother. If my grandmother had had better health care when she was younger, perhaps she would not have so many of the health problems today that cause my mother so much agony. I think if my grandmother was healthy and, thus, not in need of so much care, my mother would have much less stress. So, a shift in spending to favor the young could have positive repercussions for the young, middle-aged, and elderly.

Exploitation of Mexico

*What nations have bilateral agreements with the United States
to transfer social security earned here to their systems?
Why is Mexico excluded? What would be the effects of such
an agreement on both the Mexican and American systems?*

The United States Social Security Administration adopted the system of totalization to allow its citizens to receive credit for work performed in other countries. The system provides workers with more complete coverage when they retire, and it encourages doing business abroad. Prior to totalization, citizens were forced to pay into two separate systems— the one of the country in which they were working and the one of their home country. Essentially, they were penalized for working abroad because they were double taxed on their earnings. Totalization is frequently referred to as an international or bilateral social security agreement. The term "totalization" was created so that the goal of this shared retirement system—to add all work credits earned both in the United States and abroad—would be clear. The "totaled" work credits count toward the forty mandatory credits needed to qualify for retirement benefits in the United States. Currently, the United States holds twenty totalization agreements, mostly with European countries, as figure 15.1 shows. The first agreement went into effect in November 1978, with

Fig. 15.1   U.S. Bilateral Social Security Agreements

Country	Effective Date
Italy	November 1, 1978
Germany	December 1, 1979
Switzerland	November 1, 1980
Belgium	July 1, 1984
Norway	July 1, 1984
Canada	August 1, 1984
United Kingdom	January 1, 1985
Sweden	January 1, 1987
Spain	April 1, 1988
France	July 1, 1988
Portugal	August 1, 1989
Netherlands	November 1, 1990
Austria	November 1, 1991
Finland	November 1, 1992
Ireland	September 1, 1993
Luxembourg	November 1, 1993
Greece	September 1, 1994
South Korea	April 1, 2001
Chile	December 1, 2001
Australia	October 1, 2002

Source: SSA 2002d.

Italy, and the most recent agreement, with Australia, went into effect in October 2002. Agreements with Japan and Argentina are pending, and a suggestion to include Mexico has recently been proposed.

The totalization system is organized so that it is most efficient when the number of workers exchanged between countries is relatively equal. When granting social security benefits, the U.S. government counts work credits earned in foreign countries as if they were earned in the United States, despite the fact that the actual credits do not transfer between countries. For example, if an American earns twenty-five credits in the United States and twenty in France, the United States will allow his French credits to count toward the forty-credit requirement. The actual work credits do not transfer—records will continue to show twenty-five credits in the United States and twenty in France;

rather, the credits remain on the record of the country in which they are earned. The worker will receive benefits from the United States based on the amount of time worked (or credits earned) in the United States, and he will receive benefits from a foreign social security system in a similar manner.

At some point, an American worker must earn at least six work credits in the United States to be allowed to totalize his credits from other countries. An American may not work only in a foreign country and expect to receive benefits from the U.S. social security system. The taxes based on earnings determine the amount of a person's benefit. From the example above, the American worker would receive U.S. benefits proportional to the twenty-five credits that he earned in America, and he would be eligible to receive benefits from the French social security system for the remaining twenty credits, assuming he meets all other French requirements. The Office of International Operations (OIO) is responsible for managing the American social security program outside the United States and for carrying out the benefit provisions of international agreements.

I think that the United States currently does not have a totalization agreement with Mexico because the ratio of Mexican to American workers in the United States is much greater than the ratio of European to American workers (see figures 15.2 and 15.3). Mexico has much to gain from forming a social security totalization agreement with the United States. Many Mexican workers pay into the United States social security system, but they never complete the forty work credits required to receive benefits. This means that many Mexicans put money into the U.S. system knowing that they will never be able to collect retirement benefits. The Mexican government estimates that the U.S. government owes known recipients approximately $50 million in addition to almost $21 billion in unclaimed social security payments. When a surplus of social security taxes is collected, the extra money is deposited into the U.S. treasury. The money can then be used at the discretion of government officials for any purpose. It does not have to be used to pay retirees their social security benefits. Because the surplus deposited in the U.S. treasury is not marked specifically as uncollected benefits, the United States does not know exactly how much money Mexican workers have contributed. The U.S. government does acknowledge, however, that

Fig. 15.2   Approximate Cost of Annual Social Security Benefits

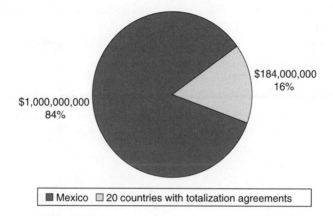

$184,000,000
16%

$1,000,000,000
84%

■ Mexico □ 20 countries with totalization agreements

Source: Migration News 2003.

many Mexican workers neither collect payments nor benefit from the social security taxes that they do contribute to the U.S. social security system. The current debate in the House of Representatives focuses on whether or not America should sign a totalization agreement with Mexico and how an operation of this magnitude would be put into action (U.S. House of Representatives 2003).

It is my understanding that the United States is hesitant in taking action because Americans will not benefit as much as Mexicans from this type of agreement. America's agreements with other European

Fig. 15.3   Recipients and Annual Costs of the Social Security Program

	Number of Recipients per Year	Cost to United States
20 Countries with Totalization Agreements	94,022	$184,000,000
Mexico	47,700	$860,000,000
United States Total	46,400,000	$372,000,000,000

countries are successful because the number of workers exchanged, and their abilities, are similar. In addition, no money is transferred between nations to pay social security benefits. Therefore, a French worker in the United States who is eligible for benefits receives his benefits from the money he contributes to the U.S. system. The French worker can receive payments from the United States even if he has only contributed to the system for six years (because he or she has credits under the French system), whereas Americans need to contribute for ten years (forty credits) to be eligible. In the case of Mexico, there is not an even exchange of workers. If an agreement were formed, Mexicans could work in Mexico for six years and then complete the remainder of the forty credits in the United States. This would make the United States responsible for paying Mexican citizens benefits for credits earned in America. Consequently, the United States does not want a totalization agreement with Mexico because it will make the American social security system responsible for ensuring that migrant Mexican workers do not outlive their money after retirement.

Countries typically have social insurance programs to protect their citizens. Because there are so few Americans employed in Mexico in comparison to Mexicans employed in America, a bilateral agreement will not have a notable positive effect for United States citizens. Mexican workers who come to the United States and pay into the social security system for less than ten years will then become eligible to collect benefits from the United States for the rest of their lives. Americans working for the same amount of time in the United States will not be eligible to receive benefits. Thus, a totalization agreement with Mexico could result in the social security system given preferential treatment to Mexicans rather than American citizens. When the exchange of workers is relatively equal, an agreement is more likely to be successful because for every foreign worker the United States helps, a foreign country will likely be helping an American to the same extent. Even though an agreement would alleviate American employers from having to pay into two social security systems, the positive aspects of this plan seem to greatly favor Mexico. Nevertheless, it is important to consider the work that Mexican workers do in the United States. Americans depend on migrant Mexican workers to do a significant amount of intensive farm labor in the United States. I predict, however, that it will take a long time before an agreement is reached because there are so many social, political, and financial factors to consider in this decision.

Because so many Mexican people work in the United States, forming a bilateral social security agreement would be a very involved process. The actual number of people that this type of contract would affect remains uncertain and may be significantly underestimated. The greatest concern about a totalization agreement with Mexico is the cost of such a large-scale contract. Congressional representatives worry that the United States may not have enough money to provide everyone with all of the money to which they are entitled. According to *Migration News* (2003), "The current 20 [bilateral] agreements cover 94,022 persons abroad at a cost to the U.S. of $184 million a year; recipients abroad receive an average $163 a month. If a totalization agreement is reached with Mexico, an estimated 162,000 Mexicans could obtain social security benefits in the first five years of an agreement." It is expected that 37,000 new beneficiaries would collect payment just in the first year of an agreement, and approximately 13,000 Mexicans who are currently ineligible due to new immigration laws may become qualified to collect benefits. Because an agreement with Mexico would almost double the current number of international social security recipients, a totalization agreement may be too expensive for the United States to handle.

Currently, Mexicans employed by American companies have to pay social security taxes to both the United States and Mexican governments. If a totalization agreement is approved, Mexicans working in the United States and their employers will only have to pay into the United States social security system, and workers will be able to receive credit for their work as if they were working in Mexico. Workers' retirement benefits are calculated and distributed according to the amount of money paid into each system. It is true that a worker does not have a choice into which retirement system he or she wishes to contribute. In most situations, there is a five-year temporary work rule that allows workers who work less than five years to continue paying into their home countries' social security systems in order to reduce transition problems as much as possible.

Another related matter that America must address is how to handle the money contributed to the social security fund under false identification numbers. It is estimated that a large percentage of the seven million illegal aliens currently living in America are from Mexico. In addition, there is over $21 billion in social security funds that cannot be distributed due to untraceable social security numbers. Mexico wants those who work illegally in the United States to also become eligible for benefits. Unlike other foreign workers, illegal Mexican workers would not be required to become citizens or even legal residents of the United States before receiving social security benefits should this proposal be accepted. There is a concern that rewarding illegal workers with social security benefits will only encourage more illegal work in the United States The proposal of extending a bilateral social security agreement to Mexico is very complicated because the full extent of its ramifications on the system is unknown and difficult to predict.

The bottom line is that a totalization agreement with Mexico will cost the United States about $1 billion per year. In addition to having to include more workers on the benefit recipient list, the United States will also have to invest money in the construction of an embassy complex for the OIO to administer social security services for Mexican citizens. Overall, the financial uncertainty of this totalization plan makes the U.S. government and the Social Security Administration hesitant to proceed.

Part III

The Economic Path to Old Age

Welfare Histories, Welfare Futures?

How many of the elderly have depended on welfare at some point?

The issue of how many elderly have depended on welfare is pertinent because social security is, among other things, a form of social welfare. Looking at the number of elderly who have at one time or another depended on welfare provides a fairly accurate prediction of social security's future. Basically, any elderly person who depended on welfare before retirement is likely to depend on social security to stay out of poverty. An important distinction must be made, however, between those who moderately depended on welfare to keep them out of poverty and those who depended on it heavily as their sole source of income. Those who depended on welfare as their only source of income did not work and will, naturally, not be eligible to receive social security benefits.

Increases in welfare dependency would mean an increase in dependence on social security to keep retirees out of poverty. On top of this, increases in poverty rates would mean less money from workers is going into the system. These do not appear to be impending problems in the future of the social security system, however. Since the 1960s poverty trends have appeared to coincide roughly with the business

Fig. 16.1   Poverty Rates, 1959–99

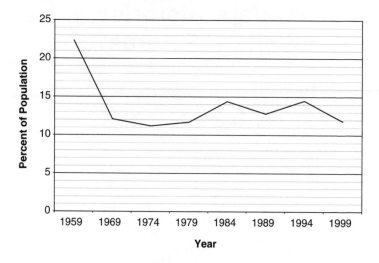

Fig. 16.2   Changes in Poverty Rates and Welfare Rates, 1992–99

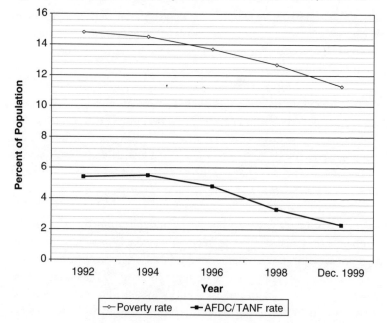

cycle (see figure 16.1). This is logical. When the economy is in a recession, naturally more people will be out of work, and there will be an increase in the number of people below the poverty level. Conversely, during periods of economic recovery, or at peaks in the cycle, there will be more jobs and more money and, thus, less poverty. In 1973, 11.1% of Americans were living below the poverty level. By 1984 this number had climbed to 14.4%. In 2000 this number had fallen back to 11.3%. Between 1992 and the turn of the century, the poverty rate fell from 14.8% to 11.3%, a decrease of 3.5%. Likewise, the percentage of the population dependent on Aid to Families with Dependent Children and Temporary Assistance to Needy Families (AFDC / TANF) fell by a similar rate—3.1% over the same amount of time (see figure 16.2). Therefore, since poverty and welfare rates appear to follow the cyclical motions of the economy, we can conclude that they will not pose a threat to the social security system unless the economy suffers prolonged sluggish growth. If that happens we will see poverty persist and become more intractable, like an early childhood disease that gets worse as the person ages and that researchers halfheartedly attempt to cure.

The Implications
of Welfare Dependency

Are those who are at risk for poverty in their early adulthood at risk when older as well?

With the current decline in the market and constant layoffs, it is safe to predict that job opportunities for the elderly will decrease as more and more jobs disappear and competition with younger men and women becomes more frequent. In 1997, 47.6 % of the elderly population of the United States had incomes below the poverty line before they received social security benefits. After receiving social security benefits, only 11.9% remained poor. Poverty in the elderly population was reduced by nearly 36%. The elderly have a lower risk of being below the poverty level and dependent on welfare than men and women in early adulthood. Yet, young men and women are now more at risk of being in poverty as they age because statistics indicate that there has been an increase in dependency on welfare over the past four decades.

For adults, elderly, and children, dependence on means-tested government programs varies greatly. Long-term and short-term dependence on Aid to Families with Dependent Children (AFDC) has gradually declined (National Center for Policy Research for Women and Families n.d.) (see figure 17.1). There has been a gradual increase in those dependent on a long-term basis (that is, those who are

Fig. 17.1   AFDC Recipients Receiving More than Half of Their Income from AFDC

Between 1967 and 1976:

Years Dependent:	All Recipients			Child Recipients 0–5 in 1967		
	All	Black	Nonblack	All	Black	Nonblack
0 Years	47.9	33.0	56.2	37.1	25.0	44.3
1–2 Years	23.2	25.6	21.9	26.6	23.6	28.4
3–5 Years	17.5	22.3	14.8	22.2	27.0	19.3
6–8 Years	8.0	12.3	5.7	9.4	15.5	5.8
9–10 Years	3.3	6.8	1.4	4.7	8.9	2.2

Between 1977 and 1986:

Years Dependent:	All Recipients			Child Recipients 0–5 in 1977		
	All	Black	Nonblack	All	Black	Nonblack
0 Years	49.5	38.8	56.2	32.0	18.9	40.0
1–2 Years	23.7	24.0	23.5	26.6	25.1	27.6
3–5 Years	12.4	15.4	10.5	14.1	19.4	10.9
6–8 Years	9.0	12.0	7.1	15.0	15.0	15.0
9–10 Years	5.5	9.9	2.8	12.2	21.7	6.5

Between 1987 and 1996:

Years Dependent:	All Recipients			Child Recipients 0–5 in 1987		
	All	Black	Nonblack	All	Black	Nonblack
0 Years	46.5	35.5	54.5	28.2	18.8	37.9
1–2 Years	23.6	22.7	24.2	22.4	21.1	23.8
3–5 Years	16.2	17.9	14.9	23.0	21.8	24.2
6–8 Years	8.0	14.1	3.5	15.3	23.0	7.3
9–10 Years	5.8	9.8	2.9	11.0	15.3	6.8

Note: The base for the percentages consists of individuals receiving at least $1 of AFDC in any year in the ten-year period. Child recipients are defined by age in the first year of the ten-year period. This measures years of dependency over the specified ten-year time periods and does not take into account years of dependency that may have occurred before or after the ten-year period.

dependent for nine or ten years of the particular decade). The majority of those who are dependent on a long-term basis most likely occupy the same category for the decades that were studied between 1967 and 1996. The trend of increased long-term dependence can mean that children and young adults have a higher risk of staying in poverty. Though statistics do show a decrease in poverty and dependence on welfare in the past, elderly who at one point or another in their lives received welfare may be vulnerable to poverty because of their inability to better their situation due to age.

Before 1996 and the legislation passed under the Clinton administration, welfare was a nationally run, almost uniform system that guaranteed those in poverty financial assistance. It did not have time constraints and disregarded the circumstances that surrounded one's poverty. Under the Clinton administration the federal welfare system was decentralized and turned over to the states. With the decentralization of the welfare system, states were able to adjust the system according to the needs of their residents and their budgets. Because of the change in the welfare system, those who were once eligible without question have either become ineligible or are now required to fulfill certain obligations, such as acquiring a job within two years of receiving welfare.

Those who are, or who have been, dependent on welfare at some point in their early adulthood now face a different system and guidelines, which vary by state and are much more stringent. Recipients remained eligible for benefits as long as they met program eligibility rules for the original welfare plan established during the Great Depression. The young adults of today who are on the brink of poverty, however, face state systems that may take more aggressive measures to reintroduce them to the workforce. The system varies greatly in each state. Some aggressive state systems can cut off welfare from those who are assumed to be capable workers. Under the state welfare systems, it seems that there is more intent to employ those who are in poverty and unemployed and who depend on welfare as compared to the older system, which just handed out lump sums to those who seemed to be in or on the brink of poverty. Those who face poverty at an early age can still be at risk, though state governments are making attempts to lessen this risk. One thing that must also be considered is the possibility that state welfare systems might worsen the financial situations of those facing poverty by denying them welfare. There is a correlation between poverty in young adulthood and poverty later in life. Thus, not solving the problem of poverty early in the lifespan can put more pressure on social security because the program is designed to replace income and also to ensure against old-age poverty through such programs as Supplemental Social Insurance.

Retirement Savings Habits

How many of the elderly planned for their retirement, and what is the lifetime average amount of money saved toward this goal? Are older and middle-aged workers ready to retire, or can we expect a retirement income security problem to force them to work longer?

In the last ten years, private savings of the elderly and retirement income averages have been steadily rising. At first glance, one would assume that this is a good thing. Social security has always done a good job, and with a rise in retirement incomes, it seems it could only get better. Using averages skews the statistics, however. When examining economic averages throughout the 1990s, everything seemed to be rising. During this time period, stocks soared and the rich got richer. This provided so much money in the hands of so few people that the average income rose dramatically. A better way to view these statistics is to look at the median because it shows a better representation of the average family. The economic status of these families did not improve, but the drop was not too substantial. However, does this drop in the median provide the average family with enough money to stay out of poverty in retirement?

While looking at the population as a whole can be useful, to properly examine retirement wealth it is necessary to group people because values vary greatly between certain groups. The groups used to assess retirement wealth are whites, African Americans, Hispanics, married couples, single males, single females, homeowners, and renters. Differences between these groups are dramatic and depict a much broader scope of the retirees.

Large differences have always existed among these groups, but the gap between the inequalities is slowly closing. When viewing projections made from 1989 to 1998 of the percentage of households expected to retire below the poverty line, the percentage only drops among African Americans, Hispanics, single females, and renters (see figure 18.1). The poverty among single males skyrocketed by jumping 17.3%, and this group became the second highest risk for poverty, behind African Americans and Hispanics. The percentage of poverty among whites, married couples, and homeowners all rose slightly. Even though the gap is closing slightly, the inequalities are still huge.

Among people ages 47 to 64 there is a surprising drop in economic status. In this group it is largely known that the average income and retirement benefits have risen. The median, though, has slightly fallen, and this causes many problems. From 1989 to 1998 the number of households expected to be below the poverty line has risen from 17.2% to 18.5%. Even worse is a rise from 29.9% to 42.5% in households that are not expected to bring in 50% of their income previous to retirement. This increase is again largest among white males, followed by homeowners, whites in general, and married couples. Only single females improved in this category. This further shows that the rich are getting rich enough to skew statistics, while the middle and lower classes are actually doing worse.

The previous data shows a trend in the male workforce that makes it seem as if the status of women is improving greatly. As women's salaries are quickly getting closer to males, this causes their retirement wealth to also be similar. While most people look at this as a good thing, the change is not actually as significant as it seems. In reality, men's wages are falling, which makes it seem as if women are doing much better when really they are not improving as quickly as many statistics seem to show.

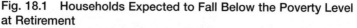

Fig. 18.1   Households Expected to Fall Below the Poverty Level at Retirement

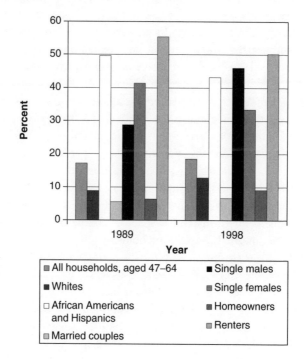

The average retirement wealth in each wealth class shows this trend. It is immediately clear why the mean is rising and the median is falling. For every wealth class below an income of $500,000, average retirement wealth decreased in the age group of 47 and above. In the wealth class of $50,000–$99,999, the average retirement wealth decreased from $242,100 to $182,000 from 1983 to 1998, a drop of 24.8%. The only group that had major gains was the class of $1,000,000 or over. The increase here is substantial, from $404,300 to $581,300, an increase of 43.8%. This drastic change was enough to raise the average, even as the median fell.

One of the main reasons for these changes is the increase in defined contribution pensions. In the last fifteen years, defined contribution

(DC) pensions have become much more common. The percentage of households aged 47 or over that have a DC pension increased from 7.8% to 47.8% from 1983 to 1998. As this happened, the percentage of households with a defined benefit (DB) pension decreased from 67.8% to 45.9% in the same age group. Mean DC pension wealth increased 959%, while mean DB wealth decreased 47%. This makes it seem as if the wealthy took more money out of DB pensions and loaded the DC pensions. As the extremely wealthy made much larger amounts from DC pensions, the average retirement wealth increased, while the average worker did not receive such benefits.

While the majority of the elderly will still be in fair economic condition after retiring, their situation does not look as promising as before. The trends currently seem to be heading downward. As a whole, the group will look good on paper, especially when looking at averages; but after close examination, it becomes apparent that upcoming retirees will generally have less money than the previous group of retirees. Luckily, most of these changes will not be significant enough to hurt most of the elderly, but it will put a larger percentage of elderly in economic trouble, which is a definite step backwards. (This analysis relies on Wolff 2002.)

Spend, Spend, Spend

*Have there been or are there changes taking place
in private savings patterns?*

The U.S. Commerce Department's analysis reveals that incomes jumped 5.9% last year, but spending has risen 7% and savings dropped to an annual low of 2.4% after taxes. This clearly shows people's inability to save money. The savings of the American people are their own responsibility. The only thing that the federal government can do is try to support supplements to social security. Forty-seven percent of U.S. households are not covered by either a defined benefit or defined contribution plan. Twenty-five percent of employees who qualify for 401(k) plans do not contribute to them.

The problem lies in the psychological tendency among many people to not pay attention to the consequences of not saving. Social security benefits now only replace 16% of the income of married couples earning $50,000 to $100,000, and the replacement rate for married couples earning $100,000 is only 9.5% of the income of married couples earning more than $100,000. America's financial myopia and its predicable capture in an excessive spending trap (essential for a capitalist system to thrive) will eventually catch up to younger Americans. By the time they reach old age, they will have no way of compensating for the gap between what they need and what social security benefits can cover.

When men and women approach retirement, consumption drops due to the predictable drop in income that accompanies retirement. Though consumption drops in reaction to this, measures to increase savings are still not taken when necessary, or when money can be saved for retirement. Researchers attribute the drop in consumption to general myopic behavior in reaction to retirement and drops in income.

Debt

How has the level of debt changed for families over time, and what effect does this have on retirement plans?

The future of young workers' retirement plans will depend more on personal savings and on the family's economy than social security. Every year there are more Americans who have debt, and this debt affects their retirement plans (Wolff 2002). Figure 20.1 shows the debt of the elderly in 1992. In that year 51.9% of the cohort was in debt, while in 1998 51.4% of the cohort was in debt. Essentially, although elderly households have not taken on more debt, over half must use their income to pay off old loans instead of using it for current and future consumption. Servicing debt poses the danger of poverty as elderly households' ability to earn more income falls while their needs increase with their improving life expectancy. However, increased life expectancy means the elderly will receive more money in benefits. These numbers indicate that the elderly are doing better in terms of their economic status compared to the past.

This prediction can be used for comparison with credit card debt but not home-secured debt. Figure 20.2 shows credit card debt vs. mortgage debt. Credit card debt usually stacks up because it has a very high interest rate. But as figure 20.2 shows, the percentage of the elderly who are in credit card debt has decreased from 30.2% in 1992 to 29.2% in 1998. This tells us that 30% of the elderly are in debt. If we compare the number of families with debt in figures 20.1 and 20.2, we find that the amount of consumer debt load influences young workers' savings. It forces people to save longer or at greater levels in order to generate the same savings because they need to pay higher debt loads. Since the debt increases with interest, workers need more money to pay debts off, forcing them to work longer. More debt means more work.

While credit card debt can usually be paid over a longer period of time—although high interest rates will rapidly increase the amount of the debt—mortgage debt is somewhat more ruthless. The fundamental rule for mortgage debt is that if the payment is not made to the bank in a specific time frame, the house will be taken away. It is more dangerous to mortgage a house than to incur credit card debt. It is extremely difficult to regain possession of a house once it is taken away by the bank. Figure 20.2 shows that mortgage debt among 35–45 year olds and those 65 and older has increased over the past few years. In 1992, 18.3% of elders had mortgage debt, but by 1998 that number was up to 26%. Similarly, among the younger age group mortgage debt

Fig. 20.1   Families with Financial Debt in 1992, 1995, and 1998

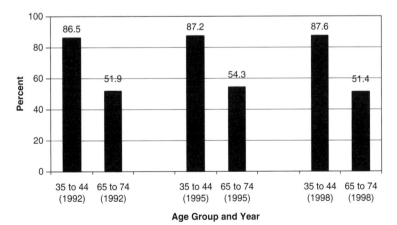

Fig. 20.2   Families with Financial Debt by Type in 1992, 1995, and 1998

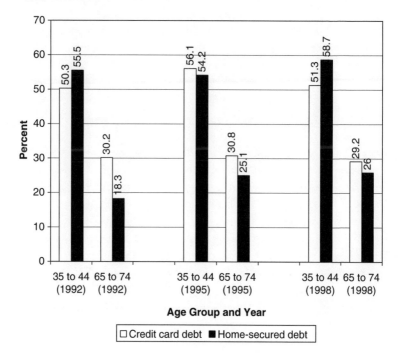

increased from 55.5% to 58.7%. This statistic shows that mortgage debt could affect young workers' retirement plans unexpectedly and dramatically (Dugas 2002).

In conclusion, the statistics in figure 20.1 indicate that the debt of young workers is higher than that of the elderly and that the amount of debt in each cohort will increase gradually each year. While 86.5% of the 1992 cohort age 35 to 44 had some kind of debt, that number increases to 87.6% in 1998 for the same age bracket. The debt of the young has increased 1.1% over the past six years. This means that increasing the debt of young workers may hamper their retirement plans.

Annuities

---

*What percentage of the elderly have invested
in annuities?*

The recent spate of corporate scandal and the subsequent crash of companies such as Enron and WorldCom have demonstrated with chilling clarity the truly precarious nature of employer-provided pensions and 401(k) plans. Hundreds of thousands of workers have been bereft in an instant of a lifetime of retirement savings. In such times of market instability and financial duress, the appeal of an annuity investment as a source of retirement income is significantly increased. Contrary to the precarious, unpredictable nature of the stock market in which mutual funds, IRAs, and 401(k)s are tenuously invested, an annuity is a stable, guaranteed retirement income. A single, well-timed investment will ensure the buyer a steady stream of income until the end of his life. While annuities represent a steady, assured stream of retirement income from which enormous potential gains may be garnered, however, there are several psychological factors that deter most people from annuity investment.

An annuity represents a defined benefit source of postretirement income as an alternative to employer-based pensions or IRA plans. As a contract between an insurance company and an individual, an annuity protects the beneficiary from outliving his savings by providing a stream of monthly or annual payments in exchange for a one-time premium. Due to the enormous potential gains from an assured stream of income, economic theory suggests that much annuitization should occur. In 1999, however, only 255,000 Americans were invested in annuities. This is because the unique nature of annuity investment prevents workers from seizing this highly lucrative retirement option.

Economists suggest there are four main psychological factors that prevent most people from purchasing annuities. First, the price of annuities is generally high. Depending on the interest rate at the time at which it is purchased and the date from which the income will begin to be collected, an annuity can easily range into hundreds of thousands of dollars. As a voluntary market, it is plagued by adverse selection, as those who invest in annuities have been shown to be more likely to have a longer lifespan. In addition, annuities entail high administrative costs. All of these factors combine to create a very expensive investment. Second, workers with the ability to "pool the risk" by sharing financial resources within a family will often not feel the need to buy annuities. Familial support, between husband and wife or parents and children, often creates a sense of financial security that negates the need for such an expensive cautionary investment. Third, most people engage in precautionary savings; they are generally reluctant to pay a large lump sum of money out of fear of an unexpected expense. Finally, most people forgo an annuity because the income it provides ends with the death of the beneficiary, and therefore survivors of the beneficiary can receive no bequest. This so-called "bequest motive" is a particularly powerful psychological motivation, as it deters those who would like to leave an inheritance to their survivors from investing in annuities.

Over the past two decades, worker participation in defined benefit plans such as annuities has fallen, while participation in defined contribution plans such as 401(k)s has remained at a constant rate, providing coverage to 50% of the workforce. Yet, despite the drop in annuity investment in the 1990s, the long-term annuity market appears to be on the rise. From 1974 to 1992 the percentage of the older population receiving retirement income from annuities increased from 18.2% to 30.2%, and over the past three years the annuity market has witnessed a drastic surge. This is due to the fact that a decline in the stock market often triggers a rise in annuity investment, and the most recent decline in the stock market in 2001 prompted a "flight to safety" investment in annuities. In the first half of 2002, the fixed annuity market surged a striking 62% compared to the previous year (Korn 2002). Despite the rise in annuity investment, the annuity market remains underinvested; in 2001 sales of single-premium immediate annuities were a meager 10.3 billion dollars (Korn 2002).

Private Pensions

Are private pension plans an important secure source of income?

The government never intended social security to be the single source of income for a retired family. In fact, the social security benefit alone does not provide enough income for most people to maintain their standard of living; rather, it was intended only as a supplement to alternate income. As a result, private pension plans, such as individual retirement accounts (IRAs), 401(k) plans, or other employer-provided pensions, represent an important addition to retirement income. However, these pension plans are inequitably distributed; only 50% of the workforce is covered by such plans, 63% of whom are workers in the highest income bracket. Low-income workers and minorities are left to depend solely on the social security benefit. As noted in the previous chapter, the recent economic recession and corporate scandals have shown the vulnerability of private pension plans. Yet, despite problems of distribution and vulnerability, private pension plans will likely play an increasingly integral role in ensuring retirement stability as the social security rate of return continues to decline.

Over the next thirty years, the rate of return on social security investment is anticipated to suffer an ongoing decline from 41.7% to

36.5%, resulting in a reduction in benefits to beneficiaries (Munnell 2003). At the same time that the value of social security is declining, the value of private pension plans is rising. According to a report from the Employee Benefit Research Institute (EBRI), from 1974 to 1992 the value of private pensions rose 6.5% (EBRI 1994). In fact, according to a 1998 Retirement Confidence Survey conducted by the American Savings Education Council (ASEC), 61% of workers expect money they save through a retirement plan at work will be their most important source of retirement income for them (ASEC 1998). To households covered by such plans, pension income is second only to social security as a percentage of total retirement assets (Munnell, Sunden, and Lindstone 2002). For a middle-income household in 1992 aged 51–61, social security represented 54.8% of retirement income, while pensions provided 22.7% (see figure 22.1) (Munnell, Sunden, and Lindstone 2002). This is more than total business, financial, IRA, and other assets combined. In 2001 the median private pension income was closely comparable to the average social security benefit, as the median amount retirees received from an employment-based plan and/or a retirement annuity was $8,136, compared to a social security benefit of $8,400 (Ghilarducci 2003).

The demographic of those covered by private pensions has been changing since 1979. Due to a drop in union membership and a loss of factory jobs, male participation rates in private pension plans have steadily declined about 5% (Munnell, Sunden, and Lindstone 2002). This decline has been offset almost exactly by the increasing participation of women, as the feminist movement of the 1960s and 1970s encouraged large numbers of women to enter the workforce. However, glaring inequity still exists between male and female pension income. In 2001, 44.7% of men aged 65 and over received pension income, compared to only 27.6% of women. Of those women receiving a pension, the average benefit was only 57% of that received by a man (Ghilarducci 2003). In addition, pension coverage for minorities is significantly less than for nonminorities.

High-income workers receive the greatest benefit from private pension plans. The value of a high-income pension plan will naturally be higher than that of a low-income plan, as a high-income worker will have contributed substantially more to the fund over a lifetime.

Fig. 22.1   Sources of Retirement Wealth for Middle-Income Households Aged 51–61 in 1992

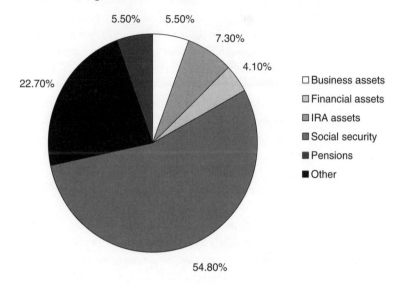

Participation is strongest in this highest quartile; according to an EBRI (1994) special report, 63% of the highest-income workers participate in pension plans, compared to 5% of the lowest-income workers (see figures 22.2 and 22.3). This striking disparity between the highest and lowest quartile is caused by a number of factors. Primarily, low-income occupations are less likely to offer pensions. Of those that do, workers often do not meet age and/or service requirements, do not work enough hours, or simply choose not to contribute to plans in lieu of a larger paycheck (Munnell, Sunden, and Lindstone 2002). Because these workers are already at the greatest risk for poverty, this staggeringly low participation rate carries ominous consequences. Without a private pension plan, these retirees are left to rely on their social security benefit as the single source of household income, a purpose for which the benefit was never intended. Without a supplemental income, these retirees are in the greatest danger of falling into poverty.

The social security rate of return is declining just as the rate of return on most private pension plans is increasing. As a result, it is

Fig. 22.2   Retirement Benefits for the Highest-Income Quartile

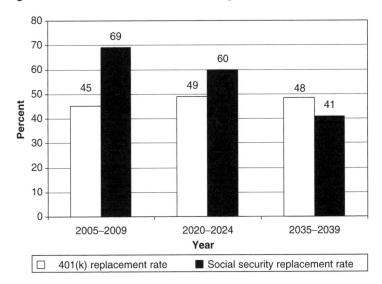

Fig. 22.3   Retirement Benefits for the Lowest-Income Quartile

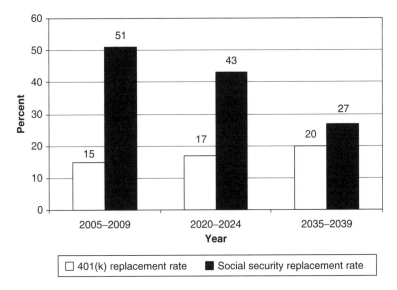

likely that pension plans will become more desirable for retirees. To simply maintain its pre-retirement standard of living, a household requires 80% of its pre-retirement income; however, in 2001 social security offered a replacement rate of only 41% to the median-income family (Munnell 2003). This is a yearly benefit of $8,400, an amount more than 50% below the 2002 poverty line figure of $18,100 for a four-person household (Bhargava and Kuriansky 2003). It is obvious that if this social security benefit is not supplemented by some other source of income, this average, median-income family will be facing poverty. As the replacement rate of social security is predicted to decrease, it is apparent that the need for supplemental retirement income will rise (Munnell 2003).

Additionally, as debate over the solubility of the social security trust fund rages, private pension income is becoming increasingly attractive as a more "reliable" source of retirement income. As politicians speak of "raiding" social security, the mere existence of the trust fund appears uncertain. According to a Retirement Confidence Survey conducted by the American Savings Education Council, 79% of workers are not confident that the social security system will continue to provide benefits of equal value to benefits provided today, while 23% of workers expect social security not to be a source of income at all (ASEC 1998). As a result, workers will turn to savings and private pension plans to ensure their retirement income.

In conclusion, private pensions represent an increasingly important source of post-retirement income. However, only 50% of all workers participate in these supplemental plans due to lack of availability or a failure to qualify for the programs. The other 50% of the workforce is left uncovered and are at much greater risk of post-retirement poverty. Of those participating in pension plans, it is the high-income worker who is disproportionately favored; meanwhile, it is the lowest-income workers, those most at risk for poverty, who are left without private pension plans. Despite the rising importance of a non–social security retirement income, the inequitable rates of private pension participation as well as the precarious nature of employer-provided pensions create an uncertain future as to the stability and availability of such plans.

A Bias in 401(k) Plans

Do low-income earners receive less of the tax expenditures for tax-favored retirement accounts like 401(k)s?

Personal or individual retirement accounts (IRAs), as well as employer-established 401(k) retirement plans, favor middle- and upper-income workers, mainly because the employers of most lower-income workers do not offer such programs. "The U.S. retirement income system is often described as a 'three-legged stool,' consisting of social security, employer-provided supplementary pensions, and individual savings," according to Munnell, Sunden, and Taylor (2000). In order to grasp how low-income earners are affected by 401(k)s, one must first understand the basic nature of such retirement plans.

According to Munnell, Sunden, and Taylor (2000), "The defining characteristics of 401(k) plans are that participation in the plan is voluntary and that the employee as well as the employer can make pre-tax contributions to the plan." This makes the 401(k) completely different from social security. The voluntary nature of the 401(k) places the responsibility for participating in and using it as a device to plan for the future on the employee, whereas social security is a mandatory social insurance system. "Since pension income is often the fault line that divides the impoverished from those with adequate income in retirement, the participation and contribution decisions are extremely important" (Munnell, Sunden, and Taylor 2000). If one chooses not to, one does not have to contribute to a 401(k).

How does this affect the low-income earners in the United States? The key aspect of IRAs and 401(k)s is that they offer tax breaks to those who hold such accounts. The contributions are tax deferred; "That is, no income taxes are levied on the original contributions and the earnings on those contributions until the funds are withdrawn from the plan" (Munnell, Sunden, and Taylor 2000). In order to receive these tax breaks, of course, one must contribute to a 401(k); however, the majority of low-income earners do not contribute. These tax breaks increase public support of government policies while they appear to cut back on taxes instead of increasing the spending of the government. 401(k) plans offer the advantage of tax breaks for those who possess such retirement accounts, which makes them very appealing to workers who are looking for a tax incentive–laden form of establishing retirement income.

In the previous chapter, we showed that low-income earners are primarily supported by social security benefits during their retirement. Thus, 401(k)s seem like a good option for these low-income earners because they are tax free at the outset and offer a secure way to plan for the future. The problem lies with the fact that most low-income earners do not have the excess income to contribute to such a plan, which is why 401(k)s are more popular among middle- and higher-income workers (see figure 23.1).

Fig. 23.1   401(k)s Win the Popularity Contest

	1983	1989	1998
% of households with defined contribution plan	12.2	28.3	58.9
% of households with defined benefit plan	68.9	60.8	43.5

Source: Wolff 2002, based on data from Federal Reserve's Survey of Consumer Finances.

Low-income workers who earn the minimum wage throughout their working lives are often employed in jobs that do not offer 401(k)s, and/or they are not earning enough money to contribute to such an account. This fact "supports the notion that workers with a taste for savings are more likely to participate in a pension plan" (Munnell, Sunden, and Taylor 2000).

Thinking Ahead

How are young workers investing their money for retirement?

Retirement has changed across generations. Today the basic notion of retirement is changing. People want to lead a life of leisure and pleasure in their retirement. Because young workers are living longer and want to spend more time in retirement, they have to start saving for retirement earlier in their working career, yet only one out of ten Americans is financially prepared for retirement at the age of 65 (Pacific Life 2002). There are many different ways in which these young workers can save money. Social security, a defined benefit, used to be the primary source of retirement funds for many workers, but things have changed. Employees are offering retirement plans that are typically defined contributions through their employers. Workers are taking things into their own hands. They are saving money on their own through either savings accounts or retirement plans that can be developed.

By looking at the increase of defined contribution plans and the decline in defined benefits plans, we can see how workers are planning for retirement (see figure 24.1). If more people today are putting their income into private pension plans and savings, then we can predict that young workers are demanding to take control of their own

Fig. 24.1   Percentage of Workers with Defined Benefit vs. Defined Contribution Plans

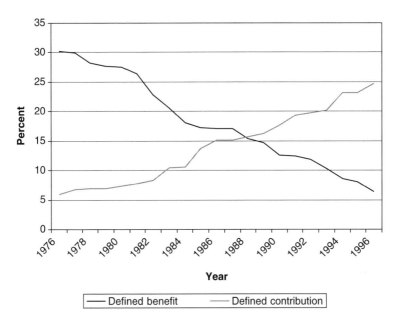

retirement plans. This is not necessarily because people do not trust the social security system; rather, they want more than what they are offered through social security. This would indicate that these young workers know that if they plan to lead a life of leisure after retirement, they have to save on their own. If the total savings is a small percentage of the income, then there are different conclusions that could be drawn. Some might say that the workers do not want to save and plan for the future. This is possible; people do not necessarily look into the future when they could easily spend the money now.

There is another scenario that could be causing these workers to save less. Maybe the cost of living at the present time is too high for workers to save for the future. If people are barely getting by now, then it becomes difficult to think about the future. It would not make much sense to save everything and live in poverty until retirement. A life of poverty decreases a person's chances of surviving until retirement;

saving for retirement is futile if one cannot live long enough to enjoy it. Many workers think this way, so much so that they do not save enough for their retirement. Recently there have been more and easier opportunities to save for retirement. With the increase in ease in saving, more workers are expected to start saving more for their own retirements.

Retirement plans are commonly offered by employers to their employees. The Employee Benefit Research Institute (EBRI) conducts studies about how workers are planning for their retirement. The reports show that defined contribution plans are rising and defined benefit plans are falling. This means that more workers are investing in plans that are not guaranteed for life. They are taking the risk that they will not outlive their money source. Surprisingly, however, the percentage of retirement wealth for the youngest baby boom females (born in 1964) shows that more of their retirement income comes from defined benefit plans. Maybe this is because women are entering the workforce later than men and they may avoid some of the risks taken by their male counterparts. The defined benefit plans do not require as much risk as the defined contribution plans. Male workers are risking more by investing in plans that are less age sensitive (EBRI 1994). This means that they can receive benefits beginning at a younger age, but at the same time, the money can run out more quickly. These defined contribution plans tend to pay out in lump sums instead of annuities. For the first time in our nation's modern financial history, more workers will have pensions to supplement social security, but since the pensions are in the form of lump sums, they have an opportunity to spend it long before they die. This accurately describes the situation that many workers will face when they retire. They have to take more responsibility for their own retirement money. The plans that they have chosen will give them more control over their money, but at the same time they must accept responsibility for their retirement planning and spending.

More workers are saving in defined contribution plans as opposed to traditional defined benefit plans. People are realizing that they need to save more money on their own in order to live the way they want in retirement. As these defined contribution plans grow, people will be able to live well in retirement unless they spend their money too quickly. It is interesting to see that people are not relying solely on social security for retirement income. People are trying to take things into their own hands and save on their own. The change from defined benefits to defined contributions shows that people are taking more risks in their retirement plans. Defined benefit plans promise workers an allotted monthly benefit upon retirement; on the other hand, defined contribution plans depend more on workers' investments. This may demonstrate that workers are willing to take more risks in order to plan for retirement.

Who's the Boss?

Are more young people employing themselves?

By definition, self-employed workers rely on their businesses as their primary source of income. While it may seem that more young workers today want to be self-employed, the numbers show a decrease (see figure 25.1). This desire to be self-employed could influence how these workers view social security. Social security will have the same benefits for them as it would for someone who is not self-employed. At the same time, however, the self-employed worker is paying twice as much into the system while still receiving the same benefit. When workers are self-employed they have to pay both parts of the social security tax, the employer's part and the employee's part. Self-employed workers have to pay 14.6% for social security, whereas other workers pay just 6.2%. Because of this, these workers may invest privately for their retirement rather than solely relying on social security. Self-employed workers also face a problem when they try to invest privately. Without a company employer offering retirement plans, it is much more difficult for the self-employed worker to invest in plans to save for retirement. This could cause self-employed workers to save money on their own for retirement or to push for more governmental aid for retirement planning for the self-employed.

Fig. 25.1   Self-Employed Workers

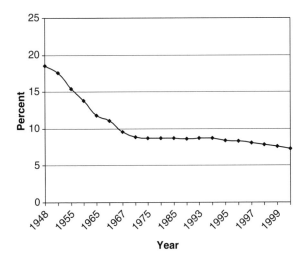

Self-employed workers face a problem with finding pension plans. Because they do not have plans through a company, fewer self-employed workers participate in retirement plans. In 1997, 79% of full-time employees in medium and large companies participated in at least one employment-based retirement plan. Only 46% of full-time workers in small private establishments were covered by a retirement plan (Devaney and Chien 2000, 31). There is not much information connecting retirement plans and self-employment, but we can still estimate the percentages. With the lower percentage of small-company employees investing in retirement plans, we can deduce that even fewer self-employed workers, who do not have any company affiliation, would have retirement plans. This creates a problem for self-employed workers: they do not have the same kind of opportunities as wage and salaried workers do for retirement plans.

Self-employed workers have to plan on their own. Alternatives to employer-sponsored retirement plans, such as Keogh plans and Individual Retirement Accounts (IRAs), were created for the self-employed and workers not covered by their employers (Devaney and Chien 2000, 32). The contributions put into these plans are tax free until distribution. With fewer opportunities for retirement plans, it appears that there are not many positive reasons for choosing self-employment. The question arises as to why people choose to be self-employed. People choose self-employment for a variety of reasons, including economic chance, achievement incentive, family responsibilities, challenge, and accommodating working hours. All these benefits encourage people to become self-employed even though retirement planning can be a challenge for them, with social security costing them twice as much and pension plans more difficult to obtain.

Self-employed workers could seek aid from the government in an attempt to save for retirement. They could suggest reforms to social security to correct the discrepancy between what they pay into the system and what they receive in benefits. They put twice as much money into the system, so it would make sense that they should get out what they put in. If this kind of reform were implemented, it would help self-employed workers but negatively affect the social security system. The money would have to come from somewhere to make up for this deficit. Though only about 8% of workers are self-employed, in 2000 there were 9,907,000 self-employed workers. This might not seem like a large group of workers, but the decrease in the amount of money in the social security system would be substantial. The social security system will face new problems if the workforce changes from the typical employee-employer system to a self-employed workforce. Thus, it is good for the system that the percentage of self-employed workers is not increasing. The U.S. Small Business Administration says that over half of all entrepreneurships fail within five years (Silvestri 1999, 15). Therefore, most of these workers will be able to invest in retirement plans through another job; however, there are still the self-employed workers who prevail. Though the number of self-employed workers is small, something needs to be done in order to help them save for their retirement.

It seems like more people are self-employed today than in the past, but the numbers tell us that the percentage of workers who are self-employed is decreasing. One could argue that the reason for this is that the total number of workers has risen at a faster rate. This could play a role in the percentages, but since 1995 the number of self-employed workers has gone down each year. Around the middle of the century it was more common to be self-employed. Corporations did not exist as predominately as they do now. People worked for themselves to provide for their families. With the rise of corporations and other large companies that are more efficient than self-employed individuals, self-employment has declined. Another reason for this decrease is that small farming has decreased dramatically in the United States (Silvestri 1999, 21). More efficient large farming facilities have replaced the small farmer. This causes small farmers to disappear from the self-employed workforce.

Being self-employed has its benefits, but many people would rather be an employee. Some people cannot afford to be self-employed; others just enjoy the benefits for retirement that employment by an employer offers.

Part IV

Changing Social Norms

From Housewife to Single Mother

Has social security kept pace with dramatic changes in family structure?

The norms of American families have unquestionably changed from what they were in 1935 at the time of the social security system's establishment, yet that has not deterred the system from continuing to meet social needs and help provide social adequacy provisions. Rapid growth in the participation of women in the labor force and a steep rise in divorce rates remain the most notable changes in the American family. But the implementation of gradual reform in the social security system has accommodated the changes in family structure, and the persistence of family benefits demonstrates that real social needs continue to be met. Figure 26.1 illustrates the incremental changes that have been applied to the system over time to address altered patterns of economic dependency. The system of today faces a wide range of critiques in relation to its family benefits policies; however, upon closer inspection, it appears that the system itself is not unjust or distributing benefits in an inequitable manner. Rather, the inequities arise as the result of a society that has not kept up with its stated values.

The social security system of today is operating as a gender-neutral system in a society still feeling the effects of its patriarchal foundations.

Fig. 26.1   Expansions in Social Security's Family Benefits

1950: Husband and widower benefits introduced (with conditions)

1956: Survivor benefits for a disabled child extended beyond the age of 18

1958: Benefits for dependents of disabled worker beneficiaries begin

1965: Benefits for divorced wives with stringent conditions

1967: Benefits for disabled widows, disabled widowers, and disabled surviving divorced wives

1972: Dependency requirement for divorced wives eliminated

1977: A divorced wife's required length of marriage reduced

1983: Restrictions on divorced wife's benefits eased further

Source: Berkowitz 2002.

Within the framework of the system, there is potential for equal opportunity in terms of economic gains between women and men; in fact, the system lends itself to the future when women and men will have more equitable roles in the marketplace. Social security reflects family values in its provisions for children and honoring of marriage as a legal arrangement in which assets are shared, but at the same time, it does not penalize for divorce. The stipulations of the system allow for the complete independence of earning women. The discrepancy lies in the fact that women typically work less and earn less. This is an issue that needs to be combated through social reforms, not attacks on a system that plays such a pivotal role in keeping many elderly women out of poverty.

Market-related work is directly subsidized through social security in the benefits paid after forty credits of recorded labor. Due to the system's emphasis on families, nonmarket work is indirectly subsidized as well through its generous spousal benefit. Married women have made the most significant gains in the labor market, making dual-earning couples the norm in the post–World War II era. A related critique is that married women boost the financial stability of the system while typically receiving the same benefits as if they had never worked, assuming that they are the lesser earner. Although this is the case, the nature of the system is social insurance, which implies that some payouts will be proportionally greater when compared to work done, but it also allows for everyone to be covered. Married women would not receive a spousal benefit if their wages were higher than those of their spouses, and the fact that more women are not the higher earners is a result of factors unrelated to the social security system. It should also be noted that married women who do work are actually better off economically when faced with the prospect of divorce, even in retirement, since they often will have their own pensions and other sources of savings.

Another accused shortfall of the social security system is that with its supposed emphasis on marriage it does not provide adequate protection of single-parent families, single mothers, or gays and lesbians. Spousal benefits are based on a legal sharing of economic assets between two people; therefore, unless legislation is passed to legalize homosexual unions, the system cannot provide spousal benefits to them (once again, a societal issue rather than a shortfall of the system). Single mothers face a very different situation, especially due to their increased vulnerability to poverty. As evidenced by figure 26.2, there has been a significant decline in the percentage of single-parent families in poverty over time, most likely due to increased participation in the labor force, but the overall number of single-parent families in poverty remains alarmingly high.

Since they typically spend less time in the labor force and often face difficulty earning sufficient wages, single mothers depend on welfare as a means of support. Those who depend on welfare most extensively receive the least social security when they become elderly; however, the aim of the system is not to provide old-age welfare but to supplement retirement income. The benefit formula of the system, in fact, works in favor of single mothers since it does not penalize years absent from the workforce and it replaces a higher share of the earnings of low-wage workers. Many single mothers benefit immensely from the system, especially those who only moderately rely on welfare, since they can take advantage of welfare during their working years and still earn enough credits to receive social security when they retire at a high rate of replacement. A vast majority of single mothers are participating in the labor force today, which not only increases social security payments but also has led to more single mothers qualifying for disability and

Fig. 26.2 Female-Headed Families in Poverty, 1959–99

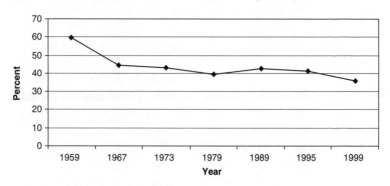

Source: Mishel, Bernstein, and Schmitt [2001, 292; based on U.S. Bureau of the Census].

survivor benefits for their children in the event that they die. Social security attempts to give these mothers every opportunity to collect benefits with its favorable benefits formula and allowance for absence from the labor force. The fact that single mothers face such difficulty collecting benefits appears not to be due to the system itself but rather the obstacles posed upon single mothers in a society where the cost of raising children continues to rise.

Social security reform has also been suggested with regard to the disparity of survivor benefits between dual-earning and single-earning couples. With a majority of American women working, the dual-earning couple has become the norm. Over the last three decades, the number of married couples in which both husband and wife work thirty-five or more hours a week increased dramatically (see figure 26.3). In 1969 both spouses worked full-time in about 24% of married couples in which both spouses were aged 26 to 54. By 1998 this figure had risen to 43%. The increase was more dramatic among couples with children under the age of 6. In 1998, fully 31% of such couples had both spouses at work full-time, up from 13% in 1969.

If the husband and wife of a dual-earning couple earn similar salaries, however, they face a distinct economic disadvantage when only one spouse survives. If their combined total earnings equal that of

Fig. 26.3   Married Couples with Both Spouses Working

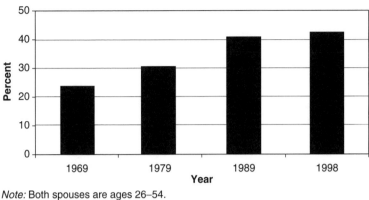

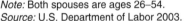

Note: Both spouses are ages 26–54.
Source: U.S. Department of Labor 2003.

what a single-earning couple makes, the survivor of the single-earning couple will receive proportionately more in survivor benefits, as evidenced by column 5 in figure 26.4. This becomes a growing concern as more women reach higher levels of education because people with similar educational attainment tend to marry. College-educated women have a higher earning potential, and a college-educated, dual-earning couple would imply a convergence of male and female earnings. This trend certainly poses a question as to whether survivor benefits favor a single-earning couple. In the case of those with higher education, however, many will already be receiving the maximum social security benefit. The idea of equivalent wages among dual-earning couples is more pertinent with respect to middle- and low-income workers. A possible solution to this drop in benefits when the higher earner dies would be to make survivor benefits a percentage of the couple's total earnings, perhaps 75%. This requires more in-depth analysis, however, and the current situation does not pose a glaring enough disparity to imply that the social security system has not kept pace with family life.

American families today are faced with the overwhelming presence of families of all types, shapes, and sizes. There are certainly people whose economic needs are not being met, and women continue to fall short of realizing their earnings potential, which can be translated into

Fig. 26.4   Monthly Benefits Paid to Four Hypothetical Couples

	Annual Real Covered Earnings [1]	Retired Worker Benefit [2]	Spouse Benefit [3]	When Married Benefit [4]	Survivor Benefit [5]	Earnings Replacement	
						Couple Benefit [6]	Survivor Benefit [7]
Couple I							
Spouse 1	$48,000.00	$1,020.00	0	$1,530.00	$1,020.00	38.20%	25.50%
Spouse 2	0	0	$510.00				
Couple II							
Spouse 1	$36,000.00	$942.00	$237.00	$1,416.00	$942.00	35.40%	23.40%
Spouse 2	$12,000.00	$471.00	$471.00				
Couple III							
Spouse 1	$30,000.00	$869.00	$303.00	$1,475.00	$869.00	36.90%	21.70%
Spouse 2	$18,000.00	$606.00	$434.50				
Couple IV							
Spouse 1	$24,000.00	$738.00	$369.00	$1,476.00	$738.00	36.90%	18.50%
Spouse 2	$24,000.00	$738.00	$369.00				

Source: Holden 1997, Table 6.3.

social security benefit potential, but the fault does not lay in the system itself. The system is based on a gender-neutral and race-neutral formula that rewards work and pays back a larger proportion of low-income contributions. When evaluating the system and determining the source of the penalizing factors, it is imperative to keep in mind its focus of social insurance and supplemental adequacy provisions. Perhaps social security has kept pace with family structure, but society has not kept pace in implementing its goals of equality.

Dependent No More:
Working Women

*How many women are financially independent from men?
How is this evidenced by changes in female
participation in the workforce?*

Financial independence in America today can be equated with earnings attained in the labor market. My assessment of female financial independence is gauged in terms of increased labor force participation rates, higher levels of education, and changes in fertility patterns. America has witnessed changes in the norms of appropriate behavior for women, and many women have emerged as economic achievers instead of as unpaid caregivers only. Rapid growth in women's labor force participation has been synonymous with female financial independence.

Pronounced changes in patterns of women's employment over the life cycle have accompanied growth in the female labor force participation (see figure 27.1). Prior to 1940, the peak working age for women was 20–24 years old, and it sharply declined after that point. "However, since 1960, there has been a sizeable increase in the participation rates of all women under age 55, reflecting declines in the birthrate and increases in the divorce rate during this period. Whereas 28% of women were working in 1940, by 1999, that figure was up to

Fig. 27.1   Labor Force Participation Rates of Men and Women, 1940–1999

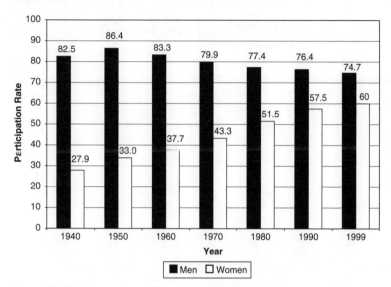

Source: Blau, Ferber, and Winkler 2002, Table 4.1. Based on information from the U.S. Department of Commerce and the U.S. Bureau of the Census.

60%" (Blau, Ferber, and Winkler 2002, 128). The increased divorce rate in America shows a direct correlation with the number of women working, but differences in participation rate by marital status indicates that married women are becoming significantly indifferent to their husband's income. They continue to engage in the labor force in the same manner as their unmarried counterparts, and due to an increased presence of single mothers in society today, there has also been a rapid growth of participation rates of single mothers since the mid-1990s. Overall, women are tending to remain in the labor force more consistently over a longer period of time.

There is historical significance behind these trends in female labor participation rates. World War II certainly played a role in boosting the number of women working outside the home, as real wages increased in the postwar boom. The period between 1960 and 1980, however, was pivotal in terms of attracting women to the workforce. For the first time, younger women entered the workforce with greater training and higher expectations. Being a working mother was finally socially acceptable, and therefore women were more likely to stay employed after the birth of a child. Attachment to the labor market also was correlated to postponement of marriage and falling fertility rates. In fact, the introduction of oral contraception in the late 1960s most likely contributed to women's financial independence, since women subsequently were more inclined to delay marriage and childrearing in pursuit of professional training after college.

Market-oriented education was largely the result of increased female participation in the labor market in conjunction with antidiscrimination legislation. Since the 1970s women have constituted an increasing proportion of formerly male occupations, especially occupations such as chemists, computer system analysts, scientists, lawyers, operation researchers, pharmacists, and physicians. Obviously, in order to attain such positions, women became increasingly educated and attained more post-collegiate degrees during the years since 1960. On all levels, the female–male earnings ratio has been on the rise, likely boosted by the increase in female education, although to this day the difference in earnings between men and women remains staggering (see figure 27.2).

In addition to disparities in earnings, female financial independence remains plagued by the high cost of divorce and the "feminization of poverty," especially among single female heads of families. Single-parent families are increasingly common in the United States today, especially families maintained by mothers. Single mothers are the most vulnerable to poverty. Households headed by single mothers have a lower ratio of adults to children, which results in fewer earners and caregivers for each dependent. Since women already tend to earn considerably less than men, single mothers face the prospect of severe economic problems. When coupled with insufficient time to devote to both work and childrearing, poverty is all too often the result. Race and education appear to be directly correlated to high poverty rates. Based on figure 27.3, black and Hispanic women had poverty rates about two-and-a-half times those of white women, and lack of a high school degree further increases these rates. Women that become single mothers after a divorce also struggle. "It has been estimated that women's income falls by 20 to 30% after divorce, even after the smaller size of family is taken into account" (Blau, Ferber, and Winkler 2002, 330).

**Fig. 27.2   Labor Force Participation by Women (Ages 25–64)
According to Educational Level, 1970 and 1999**

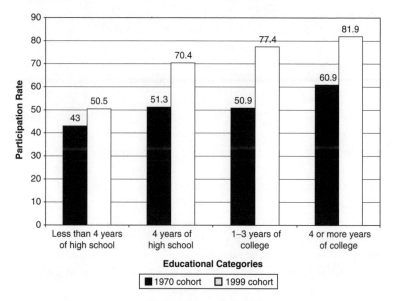

Source: Blau, Ferber, and Winkler 2002, Figure 4.9. Based on information from the
U.S. Department of Labor and U.S. Bureau of the Census 1989.

Inhibitors to female financial independence are obviously still present, but the percentage of single-mother families in poverty has
dropped by roughly 20% since 1959, largely due to the increased number of women in the workforce. Not only are more women working,
but there is a trend among working women to have fewer children
and to delay having those children until they have significant work
experience and wealth accumulation. Often the result of this delay is
continued participation in the labor force after the birth of a child and
growing financial independence. Evaluation of female economic independence using the derivatives of participation rates, educational
attainment, and changes in fertility patterns clearly demonstrates that
the percentage of women achieving independence has risen significantly in the post–World War II period and will continue to do so in

Fig. 27.3   Poverty Levels of Women 25 and Over in 1998

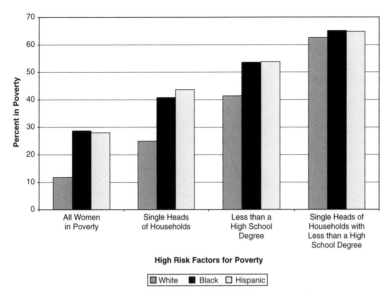

High Risk Factors for Poverty

White ■ Black □ Hispanic

Source: Mishel, Bernstein, and Schmitt 2001, Table 5.5. Based on U.S. Bureau of the Census n.d.

the future. This is not to say that all women today are meeting success in their attempts to financially support themselves, but there is certainly more opportunity for them to do so. There is no sign of an increase of women in the traditional homemaking roles in the future. Now that a vast majority of women in their prime working years are labor force participants, however, it is expected that the female labor force will now grow more slowly but certainly not decline. Women have changed the face of the American workforce, and they have transformed societal expectations of women. Put simply, the workplace is different because women are in it, and women are different because they are working.

Living Longer

How do young workers' life expectancies compare to previous generations? Are the young better off because they are living longer?

Increases in life expectancy (see chapter 3 and figure 28.1) have had dramatic effects on our social security system. Americans who live longer collect more money from social security as a result. The recent increases in life expectancy have caused the number of older Americans to increase by 3.7 million, or 12%, since 1990. Since the United States government is faced with a limited budget, the increasing elderly population will challenge the government to handle certain domestic situations (such as social security) that require considerable expenditures. Obviously, some kind of governmental policy must be enacted to compensate for the growing population. These policies can have various effects on one's standard of living. Because of technological and societal changes, it is difficult to find indicators that provide an accurate comparison of standards of living over the past forty years; however, one indicator that is not subject to these changes is literacy rates. As a result, literacy rates can provide an accurate basis for comparing standards of living over time.

Fig. 28.1   Average Remaining Life Expectancy for Those Surviving to Age 65 by Cohort

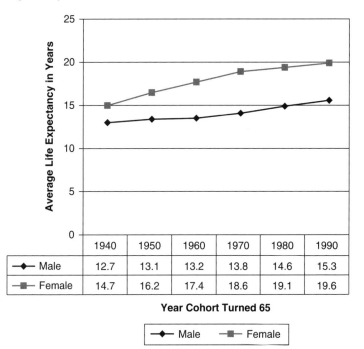

	1940	1950	1960	1970	1980	1990
Male	12.7	13.1	13.2	13.8	14.6	15.3
Female	14.7	16.2	17.4	18.6	19.1	19.6

Year Cohort Turned 65

Living comfortably is the principal goal for many retirees. There is no doubt that one's level of education can have many positive impacts on one's standard of living. One way to achieve a higher standard of living is to educate the young. Literacy rates are an important indicator of educational levels. The literacy rate is defined as the percentage of persons over the age of 15 that are able to read and write. The development of literacy rates is critical for determining how the standard of living has changed. The National Institute for Literacy (NIFL) has been collecting literacy rate information since 1992. The NIFL separated the literacy rate into three categories (prose, document, and quantitative literacy) and five levels. The first level includes people who are "able to total an entry on a deposit slip, locate the time and place of a meeting on a form, and identify a piece of specific information in a brief news article. Others were unable to perform these types of tasks, and some had such limited skills that they were unable to respond to much of the survey" (NIFL 2003). In the second level, the survey participants "were able to calculate the cost of a purchase or determine the difference between two items. They could also locate a particular intersection on a street map and enter background information on a simple form" (NIFL 2003). Adults in the third level "were able to integrate information from relatively long or dense text or from documents, to determine appropriate arithmetic operations based on information contained in the directive, and to identify the quantities needed to perform the operation" (NIFL 2003). Lastly, adults in the forth and fifth level were able to "demonstrate proficiencies associated with the most challenging tasks in this assessment, many of which involved long and complex documents and text passages" (NIFL 2003). Figure 28.2 shows the literacy rate of the U.S. population in 1992 and 1994–95. The first three levels of literacy have decreased since 1992 from 23%, 28%, and 33.33% to 20.70%, 25.90%, and 32.40% respectively. From these literacy rates, it shows that the 1992 generation has done better than the 1994–95 generation. The fourth and fifth levels of literacy are excep-

Fig. 28.2 Literacy Rates for Adults Aged 16–65 in 1992 and 1994–95

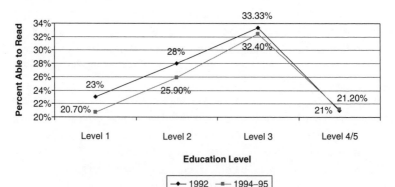

tional; the number of adults in these groups has increased from 21% to 21.20%. These data show that in recent generations there are more highly educated people, but the percentage of lower educated people is still higher. This indicates that living standards are lower because the young are not educated enough to do well financially.

Part V

When the Elderly Work for Pay

Church Ladies Becoming Wal-Mart Greeters

Will there be a decrease in the amount of unpaid or volunteer work done by the elderly?

The amount of work that the elderly do for the United States economy is underestimated. Figure 29.1 shows that the elderly account for only 22.7% of total volunteers. It is important to note that this statistic does not mean that the elderly only do 22.7% of volunteer work. We feel that the statistics in figure 29.1 can be very misleading due to three important factors: productivity, potential volunteers, and participation.

It is extremely difficult to measure the productivity of each age group. For instance, the U.S. Department of State suggests teenagers have the highest participation rates in volunteer activities because "there is an emphasis on volunteer activities in schools" (U.S. Department of State 2002). Many schools have implemented mandatory volunteer activities as a graduation requirement. However, this says nothing about their productivity. Elderly persons who volunteer by choice are likely to be more productive than high school students who are working to fulfill requirements. Many older volunteers choose to do unpaid work associated with churches and religious organizations or local school systems. Americans may not realize how important their work is to society as a whole. Oftentimes, the elderly are expected

Fig. 29.1   Volunteer Participation by Age

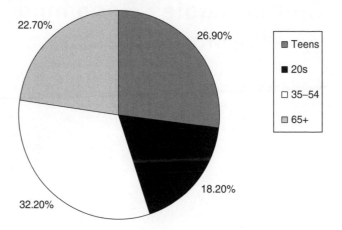

to take care of seemingly unimportant or menial tasks. According to the European Institute for Volunteering Research, however, "older volunteers bring loyalty" (Institute for Volunteering Research 2000). The institute goes on to say that "research shows that older people, who contribute more hours than any other age group, are more likely to be content with the voluntary work and stick with it." This leads us to believe that the elderly are more reliable than the young.

Second, the statistics regarding the number of hours volunteered by each age group indicate that the elderly are volunteering the most time. According to the Current Population Survey from September 2001–2002, people ages 35 to 54 were most likely to volunteer their time, accounting for 32.2% of all volunteers (U.S. Bureau of the Census 2002). Citizens age 65 and older only made up 22.7% of the volunteer labor force. It is important to note, however, that although middle-aged people are more likely to volunteer, the amount of time that they give to service is not greater than the total time that the elderly devote to service. In fact, elderly volunteers (65+) devoted a median of 96 hours in a year in comparison to the median 34 hours of 25–34 year olds.

When the elderly return to the workforce, they no longer have time to actively participate in volunteer and nonpaid activities. The number of retired people who volunteer in the United States is currently unavailable. If these data were available, then we could begin to compute the amount of volunteer work that would be lost if the elderly went back to the labor force by computing the wages for the various volunteer activities done by the elderly. Unfortunately, the U.S. government currently does not keep detailed statistics on voluntary work performed in the United States. Therefore, it is very difficult to measure the effect that voluntary work performed by the elderly has on the economy. Data shows that part-time workers are more likely to volunteer than nonworkers and full-time workers. The elderly may work part-time jobs in order to earn some extra money or because they want to stay active. Part-time work would enable them to continue volunteer work. If the elderly assume full-time jobs, however, they will not have time to devote to volunteer work. As a result, the benefits that our country receives from elderly volunteers would be severely decreased. (The data in this chapter is from the Institute for Volunteering Research.)

Elder Work and Youth Unemployment

If the elderly work more, will there be fewer jobs for younger workers? Do the elderly need to work to prevent future labor shortages?

In the short run, the number of workers is constant. Unfortunately, the number of available jobs in both the short- and long-term fluctuates according to the economy. The unemployment rate is useful when determining the present state of the economy. When the unemployment rate is high, the economy is in a recession; when the unemployment rate is low, the economy is in a time of expansion. Periods of recession are marked by a shortage of jobs, during which both young and old workers can find themselves unemployed. If this is the case, one could argue that available jobs should be given to younger workers rather than the elderly, who have already established a pension plan. Times of economic growth, on the other hand, are characterized by an abundance of jobs. In fact, there are times when there is such an availability of work that employers are faced with a labor shortage. During these times, employers are forced to hire alternate forms of labor. One major source of labor can be retired elderly. Most of the elderly do not work because of social security benefits. Thus, the elderly do not have the same motives for working as the young.

The elderly have more flexibility in choosing whether to work because they have an alternate source of income. As a result of this flexibility, employers could turn to the elderly for extra work in the event of a labor shortage.

The most significant indicator of the number of elderly in the work force is their labor force participation rate. White males over the age of 65 are the best indicators for social security analysis because 65 is the age at which the elderly qualify for complete benefits. It is difficult to compare statistics involving women or minorities because of the over-whelming societal changes that have occurred in the past fifty years. The participation rate for the elderly has steadily decreased since the late 1940s. This decrease is attributed to societal expectations regarding the accepted age of retirement. It is important to note, however, the various degrees to which this decrease occurred.

In order to determine if there will be fewer jobs for young workers if the elderly work more, we can compare the labor force participation rates of the elderly to the unemployment rates of the young for a specific time period. We were able to establish a direct relationship between the unemployment rate of the young and the overall unemployment rate. In fact, the changes in the unemployment rate of the young were more dramatic than the changes in the overall unemployment rate. The average change in the overall unemployment rate during periods of recession is 2.84%. This is significantly less than the 3.03% change in the unemployment rate of the young. We can attribute this relationship to the kinds of jobs that the young have in comparison with other age groups. Generally speaking, 25–34 year olds have lower paying jobs than other age groups. More importantly, they do not have as much job security as older workers. As a result, their unemployment rate will fluctuate more according to the state of the economy. If the unemployment rate of the young is high and the participation rate of the elderly is also high, then the elderly are working more during time periods when the young cannot find work.

Figure 30.1 shows extreme periods of recession with their corresponding changes in the unemployment rate and changes in the labor force participation rate of elderly men. We were able to find the change in the unemployment rate by subtracting the unemployment rate of the peak from the unemployment rate of the trough. For instance, when

Fig. 30.1   Labor Force Participation Rates During Periods of Recession

Dates	Change in Unemployment Rate	Change in Labor Force Participation Rate for Men 65+	Change in Unemployment Rate for Ages 25–34
Nov. 1948–Oct. 1949	4.60%	−0.90%	4.8%
Jul. 1953–May 1954	2.90%	−0.90%	3.8%
Aug 1957–Apr. 1958	3.30%	−1.90%	3.8%
Apr. 1960–Feb. 1961	1.50%	0.40%	1.7%
Dec. 1969–Nov. 1970	2.00%	−1.30%	2.3%
Nov. 1973–Mar. 1975	3.70%	−0.50%	3.8%
Jan. 1980–Jul. 1980	2.00%	−0.80%	2.0%
Jul. 1981–Nov. 1982	4.10%	−0.90%	3.8%
Jul. 1990–Mar. 1991	1.50%	−0.70%	1.3%

Source: Ghilarducci and Hermes 2003.

we subtract the unemployment rate in October 1949, 7.9%, from the unemployment rate in November 1948, 3.3%, we found that the change was 4.6%. This is significant for determining the severity of the November 1948 to October 1949 recession. We found the change in the labor force participation rate of the elderly and the change in the unemployment rate (ages 25–34) in the same way.

In order to determine if the elderly are taking jobs from the young, we decided to look at the labor force participation rates of the elderly in comparison to the change in the unemployment rate of the young during the extremes of the business cycle. If the participation rates were lower during periods of recession, then the elderly are not be taking jobs from the young; rather, they are simply providing extra labor when needed and less labor during recessions. The statistics proved otherwise, however. This becomes apparent when comparing the periods of

Fig. 30.2   Labor Force Participation Rates During Periods of Expansion

Dates	Change in Unemployment Rate	Change in Labor Force Participation Rate for Men 65+	Change in Unemployment Rate for Ages 25–34
Oct. 1949– Jul.1953	–5.70%	–4.60%	–6.2%
May. 1954– Aug. 1957	–1.80%	–3.70%	–2.1%
Apr. 1958– Apr. 1960	–2.30%	–2.50%	–2.6%
Feb. 1961– Dec. 1969	–3.60%	–5.60%	–3.9%
Nov. 1970– Nov. 1973	–1.20%	–3.40%	–1.0%
Mar. 1975– Jan. 1980	–2.00%	–2.20%	–2.3%
Jul. 1980– Jul. 1981	–0.90%	–0.60%	–0.6%
Nov. 1982– Jul. 1990	–5.10%	–0.90%	–5.2%

Source: Ghilarducci and Hermes 2003.

recession in figure 30.1 to the expansionary periods of figure 30.2. The average participation rate during a recession is –0.72%. This percentage is significantly greater than the –2.94% average exhibited by periods of expansion. The elderly are working more during periods of recession. This leads us to believe that the young are more affected by changes in the business cycle than the old. It is also important to note that the elderly who have high-paying jobs work longer than those who have lower-paying jobs. Elderly men still working after the age of 65, when compared to younger workers, have more job security. (The data in this chapter comes from Ghilarducci and Hermes 2003, which is derived from the U.S. Department of Labor 2000.)

Bibliography

Achman, Lori, and Marsha Gold. 2002. *Medicare + Choice 1999–2001: An Analysis of Managed Care Plans Withdrawals and Trends in Benefits and Premiums*. New York: The Commonwealth Fund. Available online at http://www.cmwf.org/programs/medfutur/achmangold_bn_494-497.asp.

American Psychiatric Association. 2003, March 28. "Senior Citizens and Gambling." Available online at http://www.wi-problemgamblers.org/seniors.htm.

American Savings Education Council (ASEC). 1998, September. "Retirement Confidence Survey." Available online at www.asec.org.

Berkowitz, Edward D. 2002. "Family Benefits in Social Security: A Historical Commentary." In *Social Security and the Family*, edited by Melissa Favreault, Frank Sammartino, and Eugene Steuerle. Washington, D.C.: Urban Institute Press.

Bhargava, Deepak, and Joan Kuriansky. 2003. "The Poverty Line Is an Outdated Way to Measure Need." *Milwaukee Journal-Sentinel*, January 12, 3J.

Blau, Francine, Marianne Ferber, and Beth Winkler. 2002. *The Economics of Women, Men, and Work*. Upper Saddle River, N.J.: Prentice Hall.

Consumer Expenditure Survey. 2003. "Age of Reference Person: Average Annual Expenditures and Characteristics, Consumer Expenditure Survey, 2000." Available online at www.bls.gov/cex/2000/aggregate/age.pdf.

Devaney, Sharon A., and Yi-Wen Chien. 2000. "Participation in Retirement Plans: A Comparison of the Self-Employed and Wage and Salary Workers." *Compensation and Working Conditions* (Winter).

Dugas, Christine. 2002. "American Seniors Rack Up Debt Like Never Before." *USA Today*, April 24. Available online at www.usatoday.com.

Economic Time Series Page. "Series Title: Unemployment Rate 25–34 Yrs.: SA (Thousands)." Available online at http://www.economagic.com/em-cgi/data.exe/blsln/lns14000089.

Employee Benefit Research Institute (EBRI). 1994, July. "Baby Boomers in Retirement: What Are Their Prospects?" EBRI Issue Brief, no. 151, special report.

Frew, Barbara. "How an Overseas Career Can Impact Your Social Security Retirement Benefits." ExpatExchange.com, Global Listing. Available online at http://www.expatexchange.com/lib.cfm?networkID=159&articleID=178.

Froomkin, Dan. 1998. "Welfare's Changing Face." *Washington Post,* July 23. Available online at http://www.cmwf.org/programs/medfutur/achman gold_bn_494-497.asp.

Ghilarducci, Teresa. 1999. "U.S. Social Security Reform and Intergenerational Equity." In *The Role of the State in Pension Provision: Employer, Regulator, Provider,* edited by Gerard Hughes and Jim Stewart, 141–52. Boston: Kluwer Academic Publishers.

———. 2003, January. "Retirement Annuity and Employment-Based Pension Income." Notes from class, University of Notre Dame.

Ghilarducci, Teresa, and Sharon Hermes. 2003. "How 401(k)s Destabilize the Macro-Economy and Affect Women's and Men's Retirement Decisions." Working Paper, Faculty of Economics, University of Notre Dame.

Gist, John, and Satyendra Verma. 2002. "Entitlement Spending and the Economy: Past Trends and Future Projections." AARP Policy Institute. Available online at http://research.aarp.org/econ/inb58_spending.html.

Hirsch, Pamela. 2000. "Seniors and Gambling: Exploring the Issues." AADAC Service Monitoring and Research, Howard Research and Instructional Systems, Inc. Edmonton: AADAC.

Holden, Karen C. 1997. "Social Security and the Economic Security of Women, Is It Fair?" In *Social Security in the 21st Century*, edited by Eric R. Kingston and James H. Schulz. New York: Oxford University Press.

Hungerford, T., M. Rassette, and H. Iams. 2002. "Trends in the Economic Status of the Elderly, 1976–2000." *Social Security Bulletin* 64, no. 3.

Institute for Volunteering Research. 2000. "Age Discrimination and Volunteering." Available online at http://www.ivr.org.uk/age.htm.

———. n.d. "Potential of a Lifetime-Research Summary: Study of Older Volunteers in 25 Organisations." Available online at http://www.ivr.org.uk/potential.htm.

———. n.d. "Valuing Volunteers in Europe." Available online at http://www.ivr.org.uk/euroviva.htm.

————. n.d. "Volunteering Facts and Figures." Available online at http://www.ivr.org.uk/facts.htm.

Kollmann, Geoffrey, and David Koitz. 2002, July 31. "Social Security: Where Do Surplus Taxes Go and How Are They Used?" Congressional Research Service Report for Congress. Order Code 94-593 EPW. The Library of Congress.

Korn, Donald Jay. 2002, October 1. "Investor, Know Thyself—Money Management." *Black Enterprise.* Available online at www.blackenterprise.com.

Lundberg, Shelly. 2001. "The Retirement-Consumption Puzzle: A Marital Bargaining Approach." *Journal of Public Economics* (July). Available online at http://www.econ.washington.edu/user/lundberg/Retcon.pdf.

McNeil, Jack. 2001. "Americans with Disabilities." Report P70-73, Household Economic Studies by the U.S. Census Bureau, U.S. Department of Commerce, Economics and Statistics Administration. Available online at http://www.census.gov/hhes/www/disable/sipp/disable97.html.

Migration News. 2003. "Mexico: Ag, Remittances, Social Security." Vol. 10, no. 1 (January). Available online at http://migration.ucdavis.edu/mn/Archive_MN/jan_2003-03mn.html.

Mishel, Lawrence, Jared Bernstein, and John Schmitt. 2001. *The State of Working America.* Ithaca, N.Y.: Cornell University Press.

Munnell, Alicia. 2003. "The Declining Role of Social Security." Boston College, Center for Retirement Research. Available online at www.bc.edu/centers/crr.

Munnell, Alicia H., Annika Sunden, and Elizabeth Lindstone. 2002, February. "How Important Are Private Pensions?" Issue Briefs. Boston College, Center for Retirement Research. Available online at www.bc.edu/centers/crr.

Munnell, Alicia, Annika Sunden, and Catherine Taylor. 2000, December. "What Determines 401k Participation and Contributions." Boston College, Center for Retirement Research. Available online at www.bc.edu/centers/crr.

Naifeh, Mary. 1998, July. "Trap Door? Revolving Door? Or Both?" In *Current Population Report, 1993–94*, 63–70. Available online at www.ers.usda.gov/publications/fanrr36/fanrr36ref/pdf.

National Center for Policy Research for Women and Families. n.d. "Will Social Security Hurt Women?" Available online at www.center4policy.org/sociolb.html.

National Institute for Literacy (NIFL). 2003, April 15. "Adult Literacy Rate." Available online at http://novel.nifl.gov/nifl/facts/reading_facts.html#sadults.

Occubites. 2000, May. "Career Development Center, Survey." Available online at www.buffalostate.edu/~cdc/pdffiles/occ-f-00.pdf.

Pacific Life and Annuity Company. 2000. "Retirement Planning: Introduction/ Statistics." Available online at http://www.pacificlifeandannuity.com.

Reno, Virginia, and Kathryn Olson. 1998. "Can We Afford Social Security When Baby Boomers Retire?" *National Academy of Social Insurance*, no. 4 (November).

Saperston Asset Management, Inc. "Retirement Statistics." Available online at www.saperston.com.

Silvestri, George T. 1999. "Considering Self-Employment: What to Think about Before Starting a Business." *Occupational Outlook Quarterly* (Summer).

Skidmore, Max J. 1999. *Social Security and Its Enemies: The Case for America's Most Efficient Insurance Program*, 1–22. Boulder, Colo.: Westview Press.

Social Security Administration (SSA). 2002a. "Trustees Report, 2002." Available online at http://www.ssa.gov/cgi-bin/cqcgi/@ssa.env?.

———. 2002b. "Calculations Provided by the Office of the Actuary, Using 1995 Trustees Report Demographic Assumptions." Available online at www.ssa.gov/history/reports/trust/trustreports2.html.

———. 2002c. "U.S. International Social Security Agreements." Available online at http://www.ssa.gov/international/totalization_agreements.html.

———. 2002d, October 1. "Status of Totalization Agreements." Available online at http://www.ssa.gov/international/status.html.

———. 2002e. "How International Agreements Can Help You." Electronic Factsheets, Social Security Online, SSA Publication No. 05-10180. ICN 480195. Available online at http://www.ssa.gov/pubs/10180.html.

———. 2002f, February. "Income of the Population 55 or Older, 2000." Available online at http://www.ssa.gov/policy/docs/statcomps/inc_pop55/2000/.

———. 2002g. "Annual Statistical Supplement." Available online at http://www.ssa.gov.

U.S. Bureau of the Census. 1989. *Handbook of Labor Statistics*. Available online at www.census.gov.

———. 2001a. "Census of the Population: 1980 and 2000." Available online at www.census.gov.

———. 2001b. *Handbook of U.S. Labor Statistics*, tables 1–11. Available online at www.bls.gov/opub/oog.

———. 2002. "Current Population, 2002 Annual Demographic Supplement." Available online at www.icpsr.umich.edu/8080/ICPSR~STUDY/03664/xml.

———. 2003, March 1. "Statistical Abstract of the United States Online: 2001–2002. Available online at www.census.gov/statab/www/.

———. n.d. Unpublished tables. Available online at http://ferret.bls.census.gov/ macro/031/1999/pov/new7_002.htm.

———. Various years. *Current Population Survey*. Washington, D.C.: GPO. Available online at www.census.gov.

U.S. Department of Health and Human Services. 1996. "Comparison of Prior Law and the Personal Responsibility and Work Opportunity Reconciliation Act of 1996" (P.L. 104-193). Available online at http://aspe.os.dhhs.gov/hsp/isp/reform.htm.

U.S. Department of Health and Human Services. 2002. "Indicators of Welfare Dependence." DHH Report to Congress. Available online at http://aspe.os.dhhs.gov/hsp/indicators02/ch2.htm#i9.

———. 1999. "Research Summaries: The 1999 Report of the American Workforce." *Monthly Labor Review* 122, no. 10 (October). Available online at www.bls.gov/opub/mlr/1999/10/research.ht.

———. 2000. "Consumer Expenditures." Available online at http://stats.bls.gov/cex/2000/Standard/age.pdf.

———. 2003. "Labor Force Statistics from the Current Population Survey: 1948–2003. Available online at http://data.bls.gov/servlet/SurveyOutput Servlet.

U.S. Department of Labor, Bureau of Labor Statistics. 2002. "Working in the 21st Century." Available online at http://www.bls.gov/opub/home.htm.

U.S. Department of State. 2002, December 18. "Volunteering in the United States." International Information Programs. Available online at http://usinfo.state.gov/usa/volunteer/pr121802.htm.

U.S. House of Representatives. 2003. "Lead Congressional Committees Request GAO Inquiry into Potential Social Security 'Totalization' Agreement with Mexico." Ways and Means Committee and Judiciary Committee. Available online at http://www.house.gov/judiciary/news 022403.htm.

Watkins, Marilyn. 2001, May 8. "Social Security: A Success Story under Attack." In *Economic Opportunity Group*, 98–103. Available online at www.eoionline.org.

Weisman, Jonathan, and Kevin Sullivan. 2002. "U.S. Social Security May Reach to Mexico." *Washington Post*, December 19, A01. Available online at http://washingtonpost.com/ac2/wp-dyn/A9342-2002Dec18?language=printer....

Wolff, Edward N. 2002. *Retirement Insecurity*. Washington D.C.: Economic Policy Institute.

About the Contributors

My fourteen students in "Do the Old Eat the Young? Economics of Aging" class were so fascinated by what they read in the first three weeks of the semester that they began to form their own questions and wanted answers. I scrapped the syllabus; they researched the answers to their questions, presented their findings to the class, and revised them according to their peers' exacting standards. They achieved the goals of a serious writer. The audience was not me; they wrote for those like them who need to understand. They also wrote for powerful people who make decisions affecting social security and pensions. Their work is this volume.

Natalie Bennett, a native of the Chicagoland area and an aspiring ophthalmologist, found it easy to take pride in her research. An avid reader of feminist literature ranging from fiction to psychology, she naturally researched the effects of the social security system on women and single mothers. After discovering that she now enjoys reading feminist economics as well, she eventually upheld the gender neutrality of the system. (Author of chapters 26 and 27)

Maggie Dolan is a quiet yet astute student from Illinois who took an interest in the responsibility today's worker has in providing for his dependents, whether they be old or young. (Author of chapters 13, 24, and 25)

Justin Doyle, of Canton, Ohio, is pursuing a double major in business management and sociology. He gave us a straightforward look into who is most likely to benefit from the social security system. He found himself developing a keen interest in sections of the OASDI code he otherwise would have known nothing about. (Author of chapters 6 and 11)

Carla Flemming, one of only five Alabamians in the freshman class, enjoyed contributing to this volume. She hopes that her research will help others understand the effects that delaying retirement will have on those just entering the workforce. Her interest in international travel inspired her research of the United States' totalization agreements. (Author of chapters 15, 29, and 30)

Andrew Floro calls the state of Washington home and is an aspiring architect. Researching social security required the studying of ideas that he had never thoroughly understood. With the assistance of his classmates, he was able to better comprehend aspects of the system and realize the importance of smart and proper spending and savings patterns to reinforce benefits and avoid financial myopia. (Author of chapters 17 and 19)

Caroline Geist is a native of Germany and resident of France. When Caroline attended class she brought a much-valued international perspective and an insight into the European way of life. She delved into the poverty of the elderly and came away wondering if accepted guidelines were adequate. (Author of chapter 4)

Erica Jackson, a native of Ohio's beautiful Amish country, has spent her life driven by a passion for the hard sciences, yet she is equally enthralled by languages, literature, and theatre. Throughout her examination of private pension plans and the psychological motives and scientific reality that propel them, she has witnessed within the study of economics a fascinating interrelationship between human compulsion, sociology, psychology, and biology, and their influences upon retirement savings behavior. (Author of chapters 21 and 22)

Jason Kirker, an English major and aspiring novelist from the bustling metropolis of Harrisburg, Pennsylvania, tried his hardest to determine the effects social security had upon women and minorities, particularly African Americans. He also tried to gauge the popularity and benefits of 401(k)s as they pertained to lower-income workers. (Author of chapters 9, 10, and 23)

Van Koppersmith, another rare specimen from Alabama, examined the effects welfare would have on people later in life, especially in old age. (Author of chapter 18)

Jenna Leary, a native of South Bend, is exploring a double major in economics and political science. Jenna developed a genuine interest in the plight of the elderly and wondered if increased life spans necessarily meant a better quality of life. She became particularly interested in the economic mobility, or lack thereof, of the elderly population and continually inquired into both the fairness and practicality of all our systems. (Author of chapters 1, 2, 8)

Mike Molenda, from the South Bend area, took it upon himself to examine both social security and welfare as they relate to the elderly over the course of their increasing lifetimes. (Author of chapters 3, 7, and 16)

Murf Tiawphaibul, who nearly worked himself to death throughout the semester, is a serious engineering student from Thailand. He became fascinated with debt and the ways in which it accumulates and follows one into old age. (Author of chapters 5, 20, and 28)

Mary Ursu, from Cleveland, Ohio, looked into the future to see what would be happening to contributors and beneficiaries of the social security system. She also investigated that ever-mysterious, conversation-stimulating black hole that is government spending in relation to the elderly. (Author of chapters 12 and 14)

Colin Walsh, a native of South Bend who hopes to attain a minor in economics, had his perception of the elderly's contributions to society completely transformed while studying the amount of volunteer work done by the elderly and uncovering the kinds of jobs held by those eligible for social security. (Author of chapters 29 and 30)